So You're the New Musical Director!

An Introduction to Conducting a Broadway Musical

James H. Laster

The Scarecrow Press, Inc.
Lanham, Maryland, and London
2001

SCARECROW PRESS, INC.

Published in the United States of America
by Scarecrow Press, Inc.
4720 Boston Way, Lanham, Maryland 20706
www.scarecrowpress.com

4 Pleydell Gardens, Folkestone
Kent CT20 2DN, England

British Library Cataloguing-in-Publication Information Available

Library of Congress Cataloging-in-Publication Data

Laster, James, 1934–
  So you're the new musical director! : an introduction to conducting a Broadway musical / James H. Laster.
    p. cm.
  Includes bibliographical references and index.
  ISBN 0-8108-4001-4 (paper : alk. paper)
   1. Musicals—Production and direction. I. Title.
MT955 .L37 2001
782.1'4145—dc21   2001018464

™ The paper used in this publication meets the minimum requirements of American National Standard for Information Sciences—Permanence of Paper for Printed Library Materials, ANSI/NISO Z39.48-1992.
Manufactured in the United States of America.

Contents

List of Examples

Preface

So . . . you've been asked to be the musical director for an upcoming stage production. And, your background, training, and experience leave a bit to be desired. Well, you're not the only person to have been put into this position! It has happened to many of us. We were trained to play the trumpet, to play the piano, or studied Italian art songs . . . but to be a musical director for a theatrical production? Never!

Because of your musical talents and excellent recommendations, let us pretend you were made an offer—an offer that sounds as though it will be interesting, as well as fun. Perhaps you were asked to be the musical director for a production of something like *Oklahoma!* or *Bye Bye Birdie*. And you'd like to say "Yes!" But, just what is involved? Is it really true that rehearsals last for six months? And, that they last until the "wee hours" of the morning? And, what about the audition process when, perhaps, the people trying out for a part in the show may be experienced actors and have been in more musicals than you have even seen? You know you are qualified to rehearse and conduct a choir, you can teach people their parts, so why not!

Then you discover that you are supposed to conduct the orchestra as well! You don't like batons! Sure, you can beat a 4-pattern, and you understand what is meant by "cut-time," but, what about things like "swing rhythm," "concert pitch," "vamp," or "cup mute?" What sort of language is this?

Well, don't despair . . . you *can* find help. However, do *not* expect this little book to tell you everything you need to know about being the musical director for a show. It will not begin to tell you everything that is involved. Nor, will it provide you with the single most essential element you will need to guide you through this situation . . . *experience*.

But, it *is* written by someone who faced essentially this very same situation, when he was asked to work with the chorus for a production of *Promises! Promises!* He said "Yes" to the invitation and walked into rehearsal with a great deal of confidence. Although he had not conducted a chorus for a theatrical production, he knew that he was a competent choral director, and assumed things would be the same. But this rehearsal was different, and not what he was accustomed to, still he jumped in and got his feet wet. Very, very wet!

While that first job turned out to be successful, the whole experience would have been so much easier if there had been something to read detailing what was involved in being a musical director. Or if there had been someone to talk with who could have offered some advice based on their own experiences. But, such a guide does not seem to be available.[1] Therefore, in an attempt to fill this void, this writer's goal is to share what he has learned with any who might find it helpful.

This book is directed at the person who has a music education degree with a vocal emphasis, who has sung in choirs of all types while in high school and college, or even sung in church and community ensembles, and who might have taken a course in instrumental methods in college, but who has no experience playing in a band or an orchestra. This person's only stage experience might have been limited to a walk-on part or chorus member. He might actually have no on-stage experience at all.

This book is also directed to the person working in community or amateur theatre who, like the person described above, may have some musical background, but little or no theatre experience.

This volume is also directed to the person who has some keyboard abilities and may have served as a rehearsal accompanist for a musical show at one time, but now finds that for this production instead of being at the keyboard, now he has the job of being the musical director.

This book could even be of help to the actor who may have appeared in musical theatre productions, but had no idea what takes place on the other side of the footlights when he was enlisted to *be* the musical director.

So You're the New Musical Director is not the final or definitive commentary on this subject. But, it may be of help to people with limited experience and training who are not fully aware of all the duties of this new responsibility, even though they may have considered holding the baton and conducting a performance.

And so, on with the show!

Acknowledgments

A special word of thanks is extended to Ray, who asked, "What does a musical director do?" It was this question that started the whole thing by trying to write some sort of answers to his question. Also, many thanks to all the music theatre students at Shenandoah Conservatory of Shenandoah University who have allowed me to practice on them while I was learning the techniques necessary to rehearse and conduct the many productions we have done together. A special word of thanks goes to my good friend and colleague, Dr. Thomas Albert, for his invaluable advice, as well as to those who took the time to read and comment on the manuscript: Mary Willis White, Glenne White, June Stegall, and especially my wife, Madlon. My thanks to all my colleagues in the theatre department (scenic and lighting designers, costumers, choreographers) who, by their professional expertise, have been great teachers. My sincerest thanks and appreciation is extended to Harold Herman, Director of the Music Theatre Program of Shenandoah Conservatory and Artistic Director of Shenandoah Summer Music Theatre, who also read the manuscript, and from whom I have learned so much. Thanks Hal, for giving me the opportunity to enter the fascinating world of theatre, for letting me work with you, as an actor as well as a conductor, for being a wonderful teacher, and last, but certainly not least, for being a very special friend.

My appreciation is also expressed to Tams-Witmark for materials from *Sweet Charity*, music and lyrics—© 1965 by Cy Coleman and Dorothy Fields, musical arrangements—© 1977 by Cy Coleman and the Estate of Dorothy Fields Lahm, piano reduction—© 1983 by Cy Coleman and the Estate of Dorothy Fields Lahm; to Music Theatre International for permission to reproduce materials from their publications; and to Photography by Westervelt, Winchester, Virginia.

Chapter 1

So You're the New Musical Director

In many high school teaching situations it is quite common for the choral director to find himself[2] saddled with the responsibility of preparing the school's annual staged musical production. This is either in addition to, or in lieu of, his regular responsibilities of teaching of general music classes and/or directing choral ensembles. Probably at no place in the person's college classroom-training was there any mention of the vast number of details involved in mounting a production, unless he might possibly have taken a course such as Musical Theatre Workshop, or a class in Theatrical Productions. If he had been fortunate enough to have been cast in a show, he could have gleaned considerable information through participation in the production. The high school choral teacher could go to the library for some help and find books about directing musicals, set building, and costuming. Libraries are full of material on theatrical productions. There are a few books that deal with the production of musicals. In these there will be some fleeting references to the responsibilities of a musical director. One author has addressed this lack of information by stating,

> Because of the demand for musical theater performances in schools and colleges, it is frustrating that the choral director can resort only to works written specifically for the trained theater person. The dearth of published materials for the choral director has forced a turn in this direction. The absence of appropriate materials should be remedied if choral music education is to be concerned with the musical theater art. (Tiboris 11)

The curriculum for the student majoring in music education (with a vocal emphasis) will include a vocal methods class, a course dealing with the history and philosophy of music education, some classes in repertoire appropriate for elementary or high school choirs, two or more years of music theory, probably a full year of choral conducting, and participation in one or more choral ensembles during the four years of college. All of these classes are taken along with the usual academic courses required for state certification. He will graduate having received a well-rounded education in vocal music education. If his emphasis were instrumental rather than choral, the curricular requirements would have been similar. Therefore, this new graduate feels prepared to face the world as a high school music teacher. So, what is the big deal about being a musical director?

In the hypothetical job interview mentioned above, the applicant may have been asked if he would feel comfortable being involved with the annual spring musical. Most likely, the answer was a confident "Yes." The next question from the interviewer was a little more specific. What about assuming the responsibility as the musical director for this year's annual spring production? That question may have caused you to gulp, your pulse to quicken, and your hands to get a little sweaty. But, because you desperately wanted the job, you bravely assured the music supervisor, principal, or superintendent conducting the interview that you felt quite capable of dealing with that type of assignment. It is highly possible that somewhere in your past, you may have appeared in a minor role in your own school's musical or theatrical production. You didn't pay too much attention to anything during rehearsals other than what you were supposed to do. Or, you may have helped work on the lighting crew by hanging lights with some friends on another show, but were not a member of the cast in the performances. Still this job *is* important . . . so, you answer the question with a "Yes!" and under your breath murmured, "with conditions."

You are hired. The job is yours! The class in general music is a breeze. The rehearsals with the various choral ensembles are going well. You *love* your job! But looming over your head is the specter of the spring show. Just the thought of being involved with casting, rehearsing, and serving as the musical director for the forthcoming production is making your confidence wane. What are you going to do? Where can you read something about this subject?

This same sort of situation could take place within the community where you live when an advertisement appears in the paper: "WANTED—musical director." The local community theatre group is seeking help with their forthcoming musical production and need someone to assume the music responsibilities for the show. You say to yourself, "I'd like to be more involved in community activities. I'm a good musician. Why not?" So, at the interview held at the local little theatre, you assure the director that you have what it takes to be in charge of the musical areas of the theatre's production.

Then comes the crunch! You've really got to do it! There is an orchestra to assemble (or hire), rehearse, and conduct. There may be only one trumpet, not two. The director has asked if a cut could be made in the big dance number since it is too long. One of the leads feels his big solo is too high, and asks if it could be transposed down a minor third! What did you get yourself into? Where can you get some help? Well! Read on. There might be a few answers tucked away in the following paragraphs that could put your mind at rest.

Chapter 2

The Production Team

In the majority of theatrical situations the job of musical director is one part of a multifaceted and varied group of people who make up the production team. The number of people and the membership of this team will vary depending on the situation: professional, amateur, community, school. For the purpose of illustration, we will assume that this is not a one-person production.

The ideal staff arrangement for a musical theatre production involves a production team made up of the artistic staff—the director, the musical director, and the choreographer; the people involved with the technical aspects of the production, the technical staff—the set designer, the lighting designer, the costume designer, and the props person. If the production is amplified or has any type of sound effects, there will be a sound engineer. In addition, there will be the stage manger, the cast (actor/singers/dancers divided into principals and chorus), the orchestra (or "pit") and the stage or set crew for the running of the show. There are other people involved, of course, such those in charge of selling tickets, doing the publicity, managing the house, etc. Again, how these duties are defined varies according to each situation. In this volume, only the titles mentioned above will be included in the discussion. See Example 2-1 on page 9.[3]

The producer was not listed in the above paragraph because in many amateur productions the responsibilities of the producer are combined with those of the director. In a professional setting, the producer is the person who oversees the entire production, is in charge of all things financial, and is responsible for hiring the production team, especially the director.[4]

If the list of staff people mentioned above who are required to mount a musical is slightly daunting, the suggestion by Hustoles that a musical actually involves three directors is frightening. He states that the musical director and choreographer along with the director each have a say in interpreting the creation of the composer, lyricist, and author of the show. Yet these directors and others involved in the production all "bow to the director as the head interpretative artist" (Hustoles 17).

For most amateur productions, the director is the person who is in charge. It is his concept of the show that determines the style and look of the production. He communicates this idea to the costumer, and to the set and lighting designers. Together, they incorporate this concept into the overall visual design that the audience will see. It is the director who determines the overall stage picture and decides how the actors will interpret their roles. He casts the final vote in selecting the cast, for all blocking (placing people and planning their moves on the stage), for the style of acting, and for the interpretation of the roles by the actors. The director is the final authority to any of these types of questions. He approves of the work of the choreographer and the musical director, expecting their work in the production to represent the same sense of style as outlined to the other members of the team. In other words, the director is the most senior member of the production team and represents the final word in matters of question.

In a little book published more than seventy years ago, the role of the musical director is described in these words: "The musical director should be the leader of the orchestra, or an expert pianist, if no orchestra is used. He should be competent to arrange vocal harmony and should see that the songs selected are suited to the vocal range of the singers who use them" (Hare 15). While it is an excellent trait to be an expert pianist in this business, today's theatre requires broader responsibilities for this position than were required for a 1920s minstrel show. It is expected that the musical director will be responsible for all things musical in the production: the training and/or coaching of the singers, both the principals and the chorus; working with the rehearsal accompanist; rehearsing the instrumentalists who will accompany the production; working with the director regarding any musical questions that might arise; working with the choreographer on music for the dance numbers; initiating and deciding upon cuts within the score, if needed; and finally, conducting all the performances.

The description of musical director found in a recent volume is more accurate. These responsibilities include working with the people who sing (principals and chorus) and people who play (the orchestra). In addition, the musical director

> must handle several areas of responsibility. The musical director learns the score so that he or she is conversant with the technical difficulties of the vocal score and the orchestration. During auditions, the musical director provides important input regarding the singing capabilities of potential cast members relative to the vocal demands of the show. (Ratliff and Trauth 6)

A musical director is involved with a major portion of any musical. Young reminds us that "there are four main sections to any musical: 1) lead songs, 2) company songs, 3) dialogue and lyrics, and 4) dances. Be sure each gets enough rehearsal (if that's ever possible)" (Young 2). As the musical director, you will be involved with all of these areas except dialogue. During the music learning times, your job as musical director is to make sure the notes are learned correctly. The lyrics (words to the music) will come under your responsibility when the text is set to music not only for the lead actors but for the rest of the company as well. Even though the choreographer will instruct the dancers in their movement, the actual performance of this music for the movement is the responsibility of the musical director.

The musical director is the only member of the production team who stays with the show from auditions into the first day of rehearsal through to the final performance. In every performance, the musical director conducts the show: the cast and the orchestra, and is responsible for the pacing of every performance. He is also responsible for selecting the tempo of all numbers. It should not be ruled out that the musical director may be the pianist, or part of the show's instrumental accompaniment. Even in this situation, his responsibilities remain the same since he will be conducting from the keyboard rather than from the podium.

If the job of musical director is a paid position, he, along with other members of the production staff, will receive a contract for a stated amount of money for a stated amount of time to do the required job. However, in some situations, this could be a position that is performed *gratis*. Whether or not there is pay involved, the responsibilities remain the same.

An *assistant musical director* is "to die for," and if you are fortunate enough to have a good one, consider yourself to be among the blessed. In some situations, the assistant musical director will also serve as the rehearsal accompanist for the show, provided he has the necessary keyboard skills. It is also quite common to have two separate people for these positions: one who is the rehearsal pianist, and someone who serves as the assistant conductor. In the New York world of musical theatre, it is essential that the assistant conductor (also known as the assistant musical director) have sufficient keyboard skills in order to serve as the rehearsal accompanist. In many cases, Broadway conductors have begun their careers as rehearsal accompanists and/or assistant musical directors and over the years have worked their way up to the position of conductor. Duties for the assistant musical director are many and could include checking the orchestral parts when they arrive, working with the chorus in learning notes, and marking cuts in the orchestral parts, to mention a few. If the assistant musical director has sufficient skills, he could conduct a dress rehearsal allowing the musical director to sit in the theatre in order to see and hear the show from a different perspective.

The choreographer[5] is responsible for all movement seen on the stage—either as separate dance numbers or movement/routines performed by both chorus or principals. This is an important job, as "Dance is as important in most musicals as the sets, lights, and costumes" (Hustoles 92). The choreographer will take the director's concept of the show and transfer this into stylistically appropriate movement or dance. The musical director will work closely with the choreographer, at all times being alert to whether the actor's movement will interfere with his singing. The choreographer's role is unique in that the "director has the given script to work from, and the musical director teaches music and songs already written, the choreographer must undergo a specific process to first *create* his material, structuring his dances to suit the dramatic context" (Berkson 1). Actually, the director, the choreographer, and the musical director are the people who work most closely during the rehearsal process to achieve the correct interpretation of the show.

In some situations, the choreographer may be in residence only during the rehearsal period of the production. Should a dancer or cast member have any questions regarding their movement, there is a dance captain appointed whose responsibility is to answer these questions. During the rehearsal period, the dance captain will make careful notes during all choreography sessions so as to be able to answer any questions later. The dance captain may also be in charge of physical warm-ups prior to performance to assure the dancer's body is prepared for performance in order to guard against any possible strain or injury.

The duties of the other members of the technical staff do not really affect the work of the musical director. It is helpful to know, however, what these responsibilities are. The *costume designer* is responsible for transferring the director's concept of the "look" of the show into outfits for the actors. If the costumes are built in-house for this particular production, the costume designer will prepare sketches, called renderings, for approval by the director/producer. These renderings often contain swatches of materials to be used in the costumes. At the first rehearsal, the costume designer may present his drawings for all the cast to see.

The positions of *set designer* and *lighting designer* may be combined in some amateur situations. Obviously, the set designer is in charge of all the scenery used in the production—from the initial concept of the design to the final construction. His designs for the show will be based on the director's concept. The drawings the set designer prepares of each scene will show the floor plan for all set pieces. This plan is useful to the director and choreographer as it will indicate available stage space for all movement.

The actual construction of the set could be the responsibility of the *technical director*. This person is responsible for the construction of all the materials used on the stage. He could be responsible for the crew which is to change/move/alter scenes during the running of the show. Cooperation between the director and the set/lighting people is more crucial than with musical director and set/lighting designers. However, it is helpful to know in what kind of situations the music is to be performed and if it will cause any problems. Is there going to be enough room on stage for the number of singers that have been cast in the chorus? For example, if full chorus is called for, but the set is not deep enough to allow for all of them to get on stage, that is the director's problem to solve. But, if there is not enough music in the score to cover a scene change, it is the musical director's responsibility to make sure there are no dead spaces.

Along with sets, costumes, and lights, the position of *sound engineer* is a very important position in the professional world, and it is becoming increasingly important in amateur productions. The sound engineer will be in charge of all the sound equipment in the theatre, the maintenance of this equipment, and the supervision of the sound check prior to all performances (White 17). We have attended professional productions (theatrical or rock concerts) and seen a huge console of knobs, dials, and buttons at the rear of the theatre. Usually, we see this area when it is unoccupied because there is nothing taking place on the stage prior to and after a performance or during intermission. It is too bad the audience cannot see what the sound engineer actually does while the show is in progress, for he is monitoring the console with all the skill and dexterity that one plays a musical instrument.

The position of sound control has grown to the point that the sound engineer determines whether or not we can hear what takes place on stage. He can even control how we enjoy the show, depending upon the sound level of the microphones. One Chicago production that used microphones for all the actors and for the instrumentalists in the pit, had a tragic ending due to an inexperienced person running the sound board (Myers 1999). A recent performance I attended of a London musical began with the chorus on stage setting the mood for the story. The sound level, however, was set so high that the only way I could sit through the number was to put my fingers in my ears. What a relief that the remainder of the show was at a lower, more comfortable, sound level.

In the professional world, the performers on stage, as well as the individual instruments of the orchestra, will have microphones. The sound engineer will "mix" the input from all of these sources into what the audience hears in the theatre. In amateur and community musical theatre productions there may be only floor microphones, or perhaps body microphones for the principals. There will probably not be any microphones for the orchestra. Regardless of the situation and whatever form of amplification is used, the responsibility for the control of sound will be that of the sound engineer. This person "must be your best friend. The delicate balance between supporting or drowning out the singer is in his or her hands as well as yours" (Heier 43).

A very important person with whom the musical director will be involved is the *stage manager*. Although the stage manager is not involved in training musicians, constructing sets, or preparing actors, it is the stage manager who controls everything that is on the stage as well as in the backstage area of the production. It is the stage manager and the musical director who actually run the show once the rehearsal time is completed and the show moves into production. At the first rehearsal, the stage manager distributes scores and scripts to all cast members. During rehearsals, the stage manager writes down the blocking given to each cast member by the director, sees that the cast is informed of the rehearsal schedule, relays messages from the director to other members of the production staff, and that sort of thing. In performance, the stage manager will call for the dimming of the house lights, give the call for places which moves the actors to the stage prior to the beginning of the show, calls all light and sound cues, and all set changes, including the lifting and lowering of flown scenery and drops. The title stage manager is truly appropriate as this person is the manager of everything on the stage. In order to assure the smooth running of the show, the musical director must inform the stage manager of the music cue for raising the curtain for the start of the show, for the continuing of the show after intermission, as well as for any cues during the course of the production which are based on the music.

The stage manager carries out the wishes of the director at all times. "In the professional theater, responsibility for the quality of the production goes from the director to the stage manager on opening night" (Berkson 11). However, in most amateur and community theatre productions that are only short runs, the director and the stage manager will share these responsibilities after the opening night.

The stage manager's authority is further supported by what they write in the prompt book which contains all the blocking and staging information. Whenever any questions arise regarding the placement of actors at any given moment of the production, this volume contains the answers. In the professional world, when a replacement is coming into a long-running production, the stage manager can give the new actor the necessary blocking because it is all written in the prompt book.

A flow chart based on the discussion above showing the relationship of the artistic staff and the technical staff is shown in Example 2-1.

In summary, the musical director is a member of a team, known as the production team or production staff. It is necessary for the musical director to know not only his area of responsibility, but *also* how his work fits into the overall workings for the entire production. Each member of the artistic staff and the technical staff works as a unit toward one goal: the overall success of the work at hand. And this success, "whether it be professional or amateur, will depend in one way or another upon how well this staff works together" (Engel, 1975, 2).

There was a good reason why the production staff members were mentioned before the discussion regarding the selection of the show. For the smooth running of any theatrical production, it is imperative that each person of the staff knows his area of responsibility. It may be that in some school systems and community programs, there will be insufficient personnel to staff all the above mentioned positions individually. It may boil down to a "one person" operation, with the jobs of director, musical director, and all the other technical positions rolled into one. If it is a school situation, it may be a cooperative

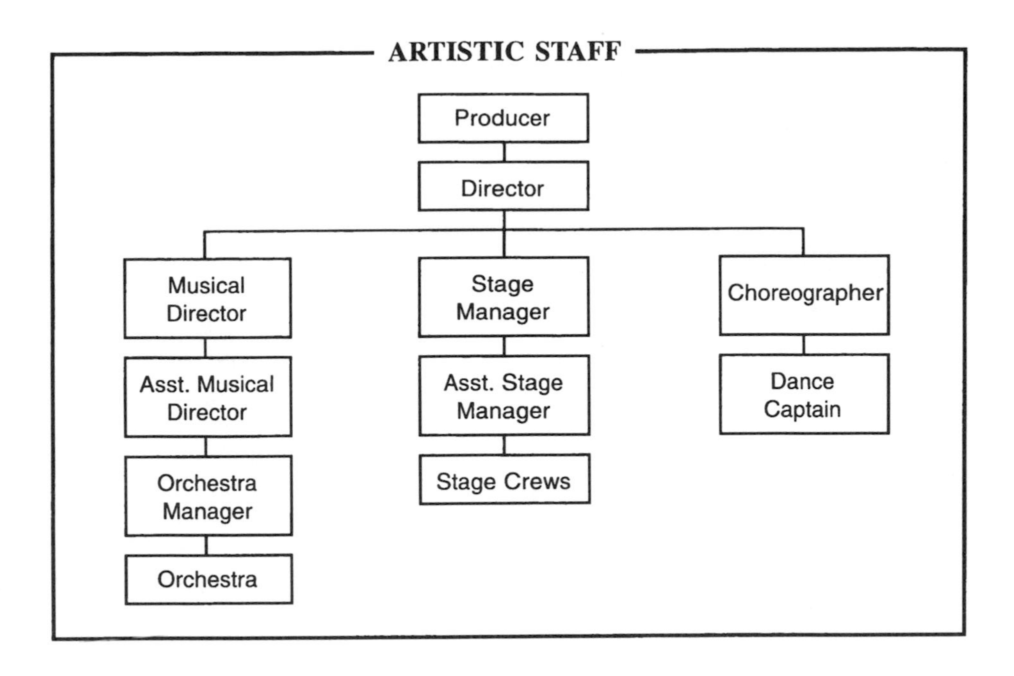

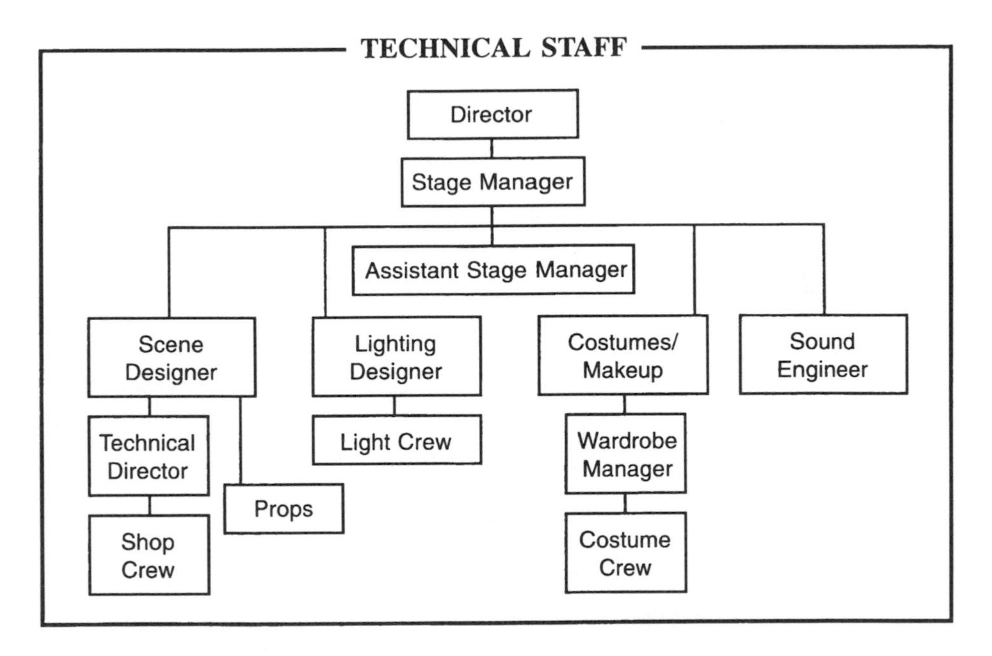

NOTE: Based on conversation with Harold Herman, 21 November 1997.

Example 2-1. Production Flow Charts

venture with the school's chorus director and the band or orchestra director sharing responsibilities. Maybe the Industrial Arts Department could be encouraged to take over some designing and construction of sets. If the choral person is serving as the director of the production and musical director combined, will the school's instrumental director adequately train the pit to meet your high standards? Who will conduct the performances? Or, maybe the school has a theatre/dramatic club person who wishes to serve as the director of the production.

Some schools even hire people from outside the school staff to serve as the director of their productions. Some community theatres have an army of volunteers to help with set building, light designing, and costume construction. Whatever the situation, make sure each person knows his duties and responsibilities before you start. In this way a lot of headaches and frustrations will be eliminated. If you are the musical director, your job is to fit into this theatre organization as easily and smoothly as possible.

The question could be raised at this point, "If being a part of a musical production is so involved, why bother with it at all?" This is a perfectly valid question when one considers the amount of time and energy expended beginning with the selection of the work through to the striking of the set and clean-up process following the final curtain. High school and community theatre productions will never attain the level of theatrical perfection achieved by professional companies; therefore, why bother with something second rate?

Several reasons counter this negative attitude, but the strongest is that of education. Taking part in this type of theatre, especially at the high school level, can be an eye-opening experience for a young person. A student's participation in one production may never result in a professional career, but it could be the first step toward a lifetime of support for theatre (Stegall, phone conversation). The theatrical business is dependent on audiences for its livelihood. Participation in one's first theatrical production could be a catalyst in the life of a young person, who will say, "I like this!" He may even add, "This is something I want to take part in again sometime." Participation, in this instance, means more than just taking the spotlight. It means learning some important traits: cooperation, because this is a teamwork situation; being responsible for yourself; discovering and accepting that there are other talented people out there who might do the job better. And these lessons can be learned whether one is performing on stage or working behind the scenes. All of these people are dependent upon the camaraderie of teamwork where the focus is on one goal—that of a successful performance.

Beyond the educational experience is the concept of musical theatre as being a living work of art, where each performance reaches hundreds of people, thousands for a show with an extended run. Art enriches life with "the good, the true, and the beautiful."

Chapter 3

Selecting the Work

It is the responsibility of the director or the producer to select the musical show to be performed. If you have worked with straight plays, you will notice that the requirements for producing a musical are more involved. That is because a musical "is an ambitious form of entertainment, since it relies upon a combination of disciplines—music, drama, and in many cases dance too" (White 1). In order to have a successful performance, these productions require larger casts, more set changes, and more elaborate costumes, along with the musical accompaniment of some type of orchestra (White 1). These factors will all enter in to the director's decision in selecting the right musical show to perform.

However, in a high school situation, since the chorus director knows the vocal abilities of the students, the musical director may be the person who makes the final selection, or is at least involved in the selection process. Regardless of who selects the show to be performed, it is important to keep in mind the abilities of the students and/or community people—both their musical as well as acting skills. You would certainly not select *A Chorus Line* as your production if you had no dancers! A few items to consider regarding the music requirements might include:

- What are the vocal demands of the entire show, for the principals as well as for the chorus? Is the vocal range of the leading role too extreme for a young untrained singer? Many Broadway shows require the use of a heavy chest-voice for the female lead singers (*Funny Girl*, or *Annie Get Your Gun*) as well as requiring the female members of the chorus to sing in the high part of their head register, especially at the end of big production numbers. Male principals usually require high baritone and tenor range. Are the singers qualified and able to negotiate the acting required in the musical under consideration?

- How important is the chorus,[6] both dramatically and musically? The size of the chorus may be determined by how many singers are needed in order to give a good sound. One will want to have adequate vocal coverage of parts, yet keep in mind the size of the stage. Can you really have a chorus of twenty or twenty-five and have any room left on the stage for a set as well as for movement? Can you use fewer singers and still provide the sound needed? Do you have enough men to balance the women?
- What are the dance demands of the show? Will the chorus members be required to dance as well as sing and act? Do the principals need to do any dancing as part of their characters? Is there a "dream ballet," such as in *Oklahoma,* that is essential to the telling of the story? Will the chorus be in two groups: those who dance, and those who sing? Singing choruses may be required to move rather than dance. Or, will you resort to that all too common practice in many productions of abbreviating the dance routines, or eliminating the dances entirely?
- What about rehearsal time? Is there sufficient time to mount the production under consideration? Is there available rehearsal space and is it adequate? Will there be sufficient time for rehearsals on the stage, or will there be conflicts with other ensembles and other school activities?
- If the person selecting the musical is not a musician, there needs to be careful consideration given to the difficulty of the music to be performed not only by the principals and the chorus, but by those accompanying. Is the accompaniment more difficult than the vocal parts? "A copy of the original score (available from the rental company) should be examined for keys, instrumentation and difficulty of parts" (Rosewall 52).
- Is the show appropriate for the age group with whom you are working? Are there a lot of character roles, or are the cast members close in age or the same age as the teenage performers? Is the content of the material too adult in nature for teenagers or more appropriate for more mature actors?
- Although not a musical item, one area to keep in mind is that of budget: What will be the expense of costumes? Can you rent them, or will they have to be constructed locally? What will be the cost to rent the music, the scripts, of royalties? What will be the expense involved in mounting the production? Will you need to build only one set; or a different set for every scene?

For the person who must make the selection of the work to be performed[7] there are many other things to keep in mind. These could include whether the person you have in mind for a particular part would even take the time to audition, much less be available when you wish to cast the show. Then, there is the matter of publicity, tickets, and programs. The list is endless! It could be that your favorite musical theatre work was the one that was just performed (and quite successfully, too) at the school just before you arrived on the job. If so, keep looking for another show, so that a recent success is not repeated too soon. But, be sure to read this next important sentence: *As musical director, most of the details mentioned above are not your concern, unless these duties have been added to your musical responsibilities. Selection of the musical is the job of the director.*

Despite all the above discussion about selecting the right musical show, the most likely scenario is that you will never be involved in this process. In all likelihood, you will be hired to be the musical director after the final decision has already been made. If it is a work you are familiar with, your job is easier because you already know the music and what the requirements of the show are. If it is a work you have never seen or heard, or it is a new work that is not very well known, your job is made more difficult because you, as the musical director, *must* know what are the musical requirements of the show before going into the audition process.

Before moving on to the discussion about auditions, another point must be made perfectly clear. No one can legally put on a production of a musical by simply purchasing the piano/vocal score of the show. This permission can be granted only by the agency that controls the performance rights of the show. In order to obtain the scripts and music for the show as well as the instrumental parts, it is necessary to enter into a contract arrangement with the licensing agency (that is the agency that holds the rights to performance), and pay the fee required for the privilege of doing the performance. The rights for performance are usually held by one of four licensing agencies: Tams Witmark Music Library; Rodgers and Hammerstein Library; Samuel French, Inc.; and Music Theatre International. (See the Appendix for addresses of licensing agencies.) Each of these organizations publishes a catalog which lists the titles that are available through their representation. Sometimes these catalogues give a synopsis of the plot, the male/female requirements, instrumentation of the orchestra, number of scenes per act, a list of best-known songs, and whether there is a professional recording of the show. Sometimes there may be a photograph from the Broadway production. More often than not, it will just be a catalog of titles. See Example 3-1.

When the final selection of the show has been made, the director or person in charge will contact the licensing agency that holds the performance rights for the show. An application will be sent which includes the name of the organization that is to perform the show, the performance dates, the number of

"A perfect classic with strong characters and humor"
—Wayne Bryan,
Music Theatre of Wichita

"Colorful characters and a bright score combine to make Guys And Dolls a celebration of the absolute best American Musical Theatre has to offer"
—Diane McFarlin,
Kaneland High School

Set in Damon Runyon's mythical New York City, this oddball romantic comedy — considered by many to be the perfect musical comedy — soars with the spirit of Broadway as it introduces us to a cast of vivid characters who have become legends in the canon: Sarah Brown, the upright but uptight "mission doll," out to reform the evildoers of Times Square; Sky Masterson, the slick, high-rolling gambler who woos her on a bet and ends up falling in love; Adelaide, the chronically ill nightclub performer whose condition is brought on by the fact she's been engaged to the same man for 14 years; and Nathan Detroit, her devoted fiancé, desperate as always to find a spot for his infamous floating crap game.

Everything works out in the end, thanks to the machinations of Abe Burrows and Jo Swerling's hilarious, fast-paced book and Frank Loesser's bright, brassy, immortal score, which take us from the heart of Times Square to the cafes of Havana, Cuba and even into the sewers of New York City. Funny and romantic, *Guys And Dolls* is ideal for audiences and performers of any age.

Based on a story and characters by Damon Runyon
Music and Lyrics by Frank Loesser
Book by Jo Swerling and Abe Burrows

Act 1: 10 scenes **Act 2: 7 scenes**

Cast
15 men, 4 women, chorus

Musical Numbers
"Fugue For Tinhorns" "Follow The Fold" "The Oldest Established" "I'll Know"
"A Bushel And A Peck" "Adelaide's Lament" "Guys And Dolls" "If I Were A Bell"
"My Time Of Day" "I've Never Been In Love Before" "Take Back Your Mink"
"More I Cannot Wish You" "Luck Be A Lady" "Sue Me" "Sit Down, You're Rockin' The Boat"
"Marry The Man Today"

Instrumentation
Reed I (flute, alto sax, clarinet, piccolo)
Reed II (flute, alto sax, clarinet)
Reed III (tenor sax, clarinet, oboe, English horn)
Reed IV (tenor sax, clarinet)
Reed V (baritone sax, bass clarinet)
Trumpets I & II
Trumpet III
Trombone
Horn
Violins A–C
Violins B–D
Cello
Bass
Percussion
Piano-conductor

Theatrical Resources

Collection

Concert Version

Logo Pack

Production Slides

Reference Recording

RehearScore™

Score Highlights

Study Guide

TV Spots

BACKSTAGE BABBLE

- *Kept from the wrestling team because of knee injury, a teen-age Tom Cruise auditioned and won the role of Nathan Detroit in his Glen Ridge, NJ high school production of* Guys And Dolls, *and so began his acting career.*
- *The original production of* Guys And Dolls *got what might be the most unanimously ecstatic reviews in Broadway history. The year it opened, it received a record-breaking one million dollars for the motion picture rights.*

Example 3-1.
Page from MTI Catalog Showing Cast and Orchestra Requirements for *Guys and Dolls*
(Used by permission of Music Theatre International)

performances, the size of the theatre, and the ticket prices. If the show is to be performed in a professional house, is it Equity or non-Equity. If it is to be performed in a nonprofessional house, is it a high school, college, or community theatre.

It can take up to two weeks before the application is processed. If the show is available (not every show is available in every location on the dates requested), a license will be sent indicating the fees that must be paid to the licensing agency. This contract will indicate the royalty that must be paid to the agency for the right to perform the work as well as the fees for the rental of scripts and scores. The amount of the royalty is based upon the size of the house, price of tickets, number of performances to be given, if it is an amateur (college, high school, community) or a professional company performing the work, the performance dates, and whether the sponsoring group is a for-profit or not-for-profit organization. For example, if the royalty is $120 per performance and you are running the show for four performances, then the total royalty amount is $480. The royalty fee is the way the authors and composers are reimbursed for the use of their "intellectual property." By obtaining a license to perform a work, you are actually paying the creators of the show for the privilege of performing their work. The licensing agency controls these performances for the authors and composers, and thus guarantees them an income from their creativity.

In addition to the royalty, there will also be a rental fee for the use of scripts and instrumental parts. This is usually around $40 for what the Rodgers and Hammerstein Library calls their "standard package" which contains twenty copies of the script and vocal arrangements and two copies of the piano-vocal score." They indicate that "additional copies of the script are available in increments of 10" (Rodgers and Hammerstein 3).

When the contract has been signed and the arrangement for payment is completed, the scripts and music for the cast will be sent one to two months prior to the performance date, unless arrangements are made for this material to be sent earlier. Rodgers and Hammerstein Theatre Library states that "Materials for amateur productions are delivered two months prior to your opening date; materials for professional productions are delivered one month prior to opening." (Rodgers and Hammerstein 3). Materials could be obtained earlier by paying an additional charge for an extended rental period.

It never fails to amaze me of the number of people who think that the "take" from ticket sales is all profit for the organization performing the show. They are not aware of or choose to ignore one of the most important costs involved: the payment of fees required for the right to the performance. Also, these same people seem never take into consideration all the expenses incurred in the mounting of the production!

The expenses incurred by one high school for their spring show will give some idea of the cost involved in mounting a production. They arranged to have scripts and scores for a three month period. The royalty and rental fee for their three night run was $1,600. For newspaper ads, posters and a photographer's bill for dress rehearsal shots they spent $350. Each cast member was responsible for his own costume which was supervised by helping parents, so expenses in this area were minimal. Still, some of the costumes had to be rented. The cost for those items, plus lumber for the set, some equipment purchased for set construction, along with other supplies ran $1,150. Fortunately, ticket sales covered the $3,100 expenses total. This relatively small budget indicates what can be expected to be spent for mounting a show (Stegall, conference).

One might ask why it is necessary to pay a fee for the performance of works whose authors are not living, such as George Gershwin, Gilbert and Sullivan, or Jerome Kern. Musicals written by these composers may be in the public domain if the copyright on them has expired. To perform these shows, you will not be paying a royalty for the use of these works, but "you must pay a rental fee to . . . the publishing company for use of all the printed musical material or buy the musical materials outright" (Boland and Argentini 14).

Remember, the musical director will probably never be involved with the contract arrangements required for the production unless he is the person who actually selects the work. This duty is the responsibility of the director or producer.

It is also the director's responsibility to make up the production calendar. This will mean reserving the stage and marking the performance and rehearsal dates on the school calendar well in advance of opening night. The director will have also made out the rehearsal schedule in order to determine the audition dates. He will decide if six weeks is enough time, rehearsing two to three hours daily, including weekends, or, if two or three months would be better? Laughlin and Wheeler have included two examples of a daily rehearsal schedule (one for a large musical, one for a small) from the first day of blocking to the final performance and the striking of the set. This chart may prove helpful to those new to the process (Laughlin and Wheeler 20-25). For school productions, the director will also have taken into consideration if rehearsals can take place during the school day as well as after school. If rehearsals can only be after the school day, conflicts need to be avoided with the other after school activities, such as athletic programs, and still have the time needed for technical matters, such as set and costume construction. One method for determining if there is sufficient time is to count backwards from the opening night, allow for a minimum of three dress rehearsals, one or two technical rehearsals, two or three run-through rehearsals, time to "clean-up and polish" after everything has been blocked, two to four weeks of rehearsals for the blocking process, the music rehearsals, the first read through, plus all the dance rehearsals. This schedule must be determined before auditions are announced for the show. Again, please remember: *this is the director's job*.

The only item not in the director's schedule which is the responsibility of the musical director is that of arranging the times for the orchestra rehearsals.

These are held separately, several days or weeks prior to the dress rehearsals with the cast. The quality of musicians you have available will determine how much rehearsal time is needed and when it should be scheduled. If these musicians are very inexperienced, you will need more time for them to learn the notes. If they are more experienced or professional players, two separate instrumental rehearsals are the bare minimum the musicians will need prior to the dress rehearsal period in order to give a confident and solid opening night show.

But, since this is a discussion about the musical director, we need to move on. Let us assume that you know who will be the members of the production team. And, as musical director, you know your duties. And, let us assume that the director has selected the ideal show. It is now time to see and hear the people who want to be in the show!

Chapter 4

Auditions

The show has been selected, the staff is set, and you are ready to see the people who would like to be a part of this production. The director will want to make an announcement to the entire school giving information about the forthcoming production. If it is a community-oriented project, announcements can be placed in the local paper, in order to get the word out to interested residents. If the production is within the school environment, posters should be displayed announcing the name of the production, when and where auditions will take place, as well as announcements in bulletins that teachers read to their classes. Email can be very helpful in sending fast messages electronically if you have the names of club members, chorus members, and the community theatre membership in group files. The school library is a good location for scripts and scores, maybe even a recording if one is available, to be placed where they will be accessible to all people interested in auditioning. Having these materials available will allow for time for reading the script and listening to the music prior to the audition. A person might discover a special part they would like to be considered for. If there are specific audition requirements (accents, character parts), be sure to announce these early, should special preparation be necessary.

As the school choral director, you may already know who you think would be the best person to play a particular part, based upon their musical skills. But, the final casting decision is a team effort, and who knows what surprises may be waiting. Plus, students are very busy with other activities and there will be conflicts between rehearsals/performances of your production with sports, field trips, and other school activities. And the singer in your choir that you think would be good for a part may not have time for this extracurricular activity. Do not forget the schedules of people who are in the business world and who would like to take part in the community production, too. Their world cannot stop just because a musical is about to be cast! It never fails that the person just right for a particular part is involved in other school activities. Or there is an ideal person available for the community theatre production who will be away on a business trip on opening night! Miller cautions that in high school productions,

> I have found that the person you want in the cast is usually among the busiest in school. These people are in orchestras and choruses, on the staffs of the Annual or the school newspaper, and are members of student councils and officers in school clubs. But, be sure, *be very sure*, that such a student is going to be free for rehearsals. (L. Miller 17)

The directing team (the director, the musical director, and the choreographer) will be present to hear the auditions. It is absolutely necessary that every person auditioning sing individually, even if you have heard them daily in your chorus all year long, or in your church choir every Sunday.

Information should be available prior to the audition time indicating what each actor is expected to do. For example, do you want them to sing a selection from the production? Do you want them to sing something of their own choosing? Or will you require them to perform music you have selected? Whatever the method, you will not want to sit through a long performance by any singer. Auditions would take forever if you did. To save time, suggest that each person sing sixteen to twenty-four measures of a song of their choice that best shows their vocal capabilities. Many professional auditions require two songs of contrasting style—a ballad and an up-tempo number. This allows the females to show both their "legit voice" as well as their "belt voice." Some professional auditions even require a song to be read at sight. By limiting the duration of the music to be sung, you will encourage the auditionees to show the directing team their highest note, their loudest note, and their prettiest note, as well as how well they can "sell" a song.

When audition times are posted, the director should indicate if the actors are required to do a dance/movement audition at the same time. Many advertisements just include, "be prepared to move," or "wear comfortable clothing for dance." Many actors will dress professionally for their singing and monolog audition portion, and will bring clothing suitable for moving (dance leotards and dance shoes) into which they can change after the singing portion of the audition is completed. The dance part of the audition is the time when the choreographer will have each person learn and perform a simple dance combination. This combination might be in the style of one of the numbers that will be danced in the show. It should not be so difficult that it will take hours to learn, or so long that it will prevent you from seeing all of the people there to audition. But the dance audition should show whether the person can move and how quick they are at picking up dance steps and combinations.

Your job as musical director is to listen to the voice, because in your job you are interested in the vocal aspect of the actor. You will be concerned not only with the quality of the sound, but with accuracy of pitch and with their vocal range. You will be concerned about the singer's ability to project in the size room where the performance will be held, as well as the ability to project over an instrumental accompaniment. But most importantly, you will be listening to determine if the voice seems to be especially appropriate for a particular character in the show the actor would like to be considered for.

Audition time is where the director should enlist the assistance of one or more helpers. These people could be students if a school production, or volunteers from the area if it is a community theatre production. They can monitor the sign-in table, and give out the cards for each person to fill out. If the students have been involved in the audition process before, they can answer the many questions that the nervous candidates might have. When the actors enter the audition area, have each person fill out a card giving information such as name, age, address, and what part in the show they wish to be considered for: a principal role or chorus. They may have no preference for a part. If this is the case, they should write "as cast" on the card indicating they will accept whatever the director assigns. It might be a good idea to have them give you some information about their previous stage experience.

At professional auditions, each person auditioning must provide the director with a photograph (called a head-shot) or a composite (photographs showing them in various roles) along with their resume (a list of their previous theatrical experience) attached to the back. When the announcement for the show has been made, an actor wishing to be considered for a part will call asking for an audition time. When the date and time have been secured, the actor will send a copy of his headshot/resume (abbreviated as H/R or P/R for photo/resume). At the audition time, the director will have these in order on his table and will make notes on them. Or, the actor will bring his headshot/resume with him at the audition time and give it to the assistant when signing in or to the director at the time of the audition. Most professional auditions are arranged through the actor's agent. The director and producer announce the show and the cast requirements. Agents submit photos and resumes for consideration. The director and producer select from the information submitted and call in people they wish to see and hear.

In community and amateur theatre, the process may be just an announcement in the paper and anyone wishing to audition should show up and sing or read from the script. In these situations, a headshot/resume may or may not be required. However, if the actor has H/R copies available, bring them to the audition. Better to be prepared.

Individual Auditions

A group of people has assembled and are waiting to audition. Auditions usually go in order from the first person to sign in, and ending with the last to arrive. Each person is given a number or some indication as to what the order of each audition will be. When the person's name or number is called, they will give their card to the director (or person in charge of the auditions). Then, they should take their music to the accompanist. It will only take a minute or less to set the tempo, whether or not to take repeats, and that sort of thing. This is not your problem as musical director, but in case someone should ask about audition procedures, you can inform them about correct etiquette in this area. This same routine is quite similar in amateur and professional theatre. Some auditions have actors appear in groups, but audition individually. Other places have the actors wait in a separate room until called into the audition area. When their name is called, they will present their card or photo/resume to the director and then give the accompanist their music telling them the tempo.

It is important that the accompanist feel comfortable with the singer as well as for the singer to feel confident that the accompanist will provide the necessary support. Bruce Miller's suggestions for making the accompanist's job easy and more helpful to you are invaluable. "To begin with," writes Miller,

> you can put your accompanist at ease by arranging the music in a loose-leave binder, or by taping the song pages in such a way that she can spread it across the piano stand easily. Do not expect the accompanist to be able to transpose your song. If you want a particular note to be played, it should read that way on the page. Any tempo changes or other musical variations should be marked clearly on the score and pointed out if possible. It is your responsibility to discuss with your accompanist when she is to begin playing and the exact manner in which you will let her know. (27)

While the actor is talking with the accompanist, the people hearing the audition can have time to look over the card that has been filled out, or look at the headshot and read the resume. Another audition procedure is to have the actors present their card and headshots/resumes to an assistant at the sign-in time. The assistant will take them to the director, who will then decide what order the individuals in the group will be called to audition. This method is often done when they are hearing a group of people auditioning for a single part.

When the person is ready to sing, he should step into the audition space which could be a rehearsal room or stage. He will clearly state his name and the title of the selection he will sing. The actor should nod to the accompanist, who will begin the introduction in the agreed upon tempo or give a starting pitch. Then, the actor sings his prepared selection. If a monolog is to be performed at the audition time, the actor should announce the titles of each and go directly from the song into the monolog. It is acceptable to give the title before each of the audition selections.

When the audition is completed, the actor says "thank you" to the production team and leaves the audition space. It is a courtesy to say "thank you" to the accompanist as he collects his music.

The director will probably make his personal notes on the card, on the resume, or on a separate piece of paper, as the person is performing. As musical director, you will want to make your own notes on a separate form which you have prepared in advance and list only the qualities you are interested in, so you can quickly check them off, or make comments in the appropriate areas.

During each audition, be sure to keep your eyes directly on the person as they sing. Notice their facial expression. Notice how they hold their body. Is there any evidence of tension? Are they so frightened that they can barely make a sound, or does the person move freely to the music and in character to the mood of the song? It does not take a lot of training to notice these qualities. Your notations can be made quickly on the card or form that you have prepared. It will not take long before you will be able to assess the quality of each auditionee within a matter of seconds. Granted the more experience you have in hearing people the easier the task.

You will not expect the person auditioning to make eye contact with any of the people hearing the audition. Just as you would not want to make eye contact with a member of the audience during a performance, the auditionee should perform in the same vein. Fred Silver has made a list of guidelines to help actors do their best. He suggests that this list may be referred to as the "Ten Commandments of Auditioning for a Musical." Item number six cautions the actors to "avoid making eye contact with your auditors: they are not your acting partners. Rather they are voyeurs watching you give a performance to an imaginary partner" (Silver 1989, 95). Silver's list should be required reading for anyone auditioning for musical theatre. If you are working with students with little or no experience, you might be asked about audition requirements, expectations, and etiquette. It would be good to suggest to your young actors that they read these "Ten Commandments" or even post this list in your classroom area.

Even if you are new to the audition process, you will quickly notice a variety of performance levels. Some people just stand and sing a song, while others instantly communicate what they are thinking or singing. They seem to take over the situation in presenting themselves to you. They have that magic which can cross the footlights and carry the message to the back row of the theatre. One author reflecting on community theatre auditions observed this magic in a particular actor after a long day of auditions. "From the second she opens her mouth, everyone at the table sits up straight. Every move she makes is like water pouring from an elegant pitcher—smooth, direct, refreshing" (Fisher 5). And no two performers are the same. Even when the same vocal selection is performed by two different people, it will become two totally different renditions.

But how are you going to remember all these faces and their sounds? If facilities allow, the use of a video recorder to tape the audition is an easy and accurate reference after everyone has finished auditioning. This would be especially helpful if there are a lot of people to hear. However, a video device should be used with caution as the presence of the camera or a microphone may make the inexperienced auditionee more uncomfortable than he already is.

One way of keeping track of a large number of auditionees that works for me is to make a simple list on a legal pad. The number next to the name corresponds to the order of appearance. Besides each name, I write the title of the musical selection as it is announced by the actor. In addition to name and selection, I quickly jot down terse observations, such as: nasal, good pitch, small voice, lyrical sound, confident, big voice, frightened. I write any verbal description of the voice and the person's delivery that will aid in recalling how the actor performed. Each person is rated on a scale of one to five, with one being the highest mark. It is essential that you have some way to remember the person when you later meet with the director and choreographer at the casting meeting, whether it be immediately following auditions or days later. With these notes you have a fairly accurate survey with which to make your contribution to the casting process. Sometimes it is helpful to make some comment regarding height, build, hair style, or even what they were wearing. You want to provide yourself with any clues that will assist in deciding which actors to hear at call-backs, or in making the final casting decisions.[8]

If monologs are a part of the audition process, I rate these as well, using a rating scale of A, B, C with a plus and minus. By making the musical ratings Arabic numbers and the monolog ratings capital letters, the two are kept

		Auditions for Beach Journey	
		30 January 2000	
Dance	Rating		Monolog
II+	3+	1. Paula Davidson "Tonight" WSS long hair, yellow sweater soprano, pitch OK, good diction, not much energy	B+
I-	1-	2. Jerry Culp "Wilkommen" (Cabaret) nice tenor, good sense of style, high energy, good projection	A-
I+	4	3. Megan Thomas "Meadowlark" reedy, breathy sound, pronounced break	C
———	>>>>	———>>>>———>>>>———>>>>———>>>>	———
III	1	55. Aaron Williams "Where's the Girl" killer smile very pleasing baritone, good use of top register, excellent diction	B
II	2+	56. Katie Schmaltz "How Could I Ever Know" lyrical, clear sound, light soprano, not a big voice	A+
I	1★	57. Brenda Davis "Always True to You, Darlin'" a bright belt, able to mix top register, sells song!	A-

Example 4-1. Sample Audition List

separate. I also rate the dance audition, but for this I use Roman numerals, I, II, III, also with plus and minus indications.

What is the most efficient use of time at auditions when you have people sing and learn a dance combination? Do you have the dancers audition individually or in groups? One way to conduct the audition is to have eight to ten people sing. Then have the choreographer teach a dance combination to the people who have already sung. The musical director and director will watch the people dance and make their own comments on their card or sheet. When this dance portion is completed, and each person has been evaluated on their movement abilities, the auditions continue with another group of people who sing, then dance.

Another audition procedure would be to have all the actors sing. When all have sung, then have everyone dance. If the choreographer has worked with any of the auditionees previously, these people might be excused from the dance part of the audition keeping only those whose dancing ability is unknown or those in question, to learn the combination. If there are a lot of people auditioning, two separate locations might be used: one for singing, one for dancing. The choreographer will want to keep records on each person's abilities and give them a rating on some sort of scale as the musical director and the director do. Many times in auditions the choreographer will have made comments regarding the singing or reading of an actor that has been extremely helpful at the casting meeting. This is an example of the team approach.

Auditions can take a long time, but you want to be sure that everyone who comes to the auditions has a fair chance to show you the very best they have to offer. Therefore, patience is a virtue! The production team wants each person to give the strongest and best audition they are capable of doing. There can be tension and nervousness on both sides of the table: for the actors presenting themselves to the auditioners, and concern by the people hearing the audition about the time it takes and the desire to have the right person selected for the various roles.

A word might be injected here regarding audition manners. "No matter how experienced an actor may be, auditioning can still be a nerve-wracking experience. It is important that the production team recognize this, and treat each auditionee with courtesy and respect" (White 53). The team's job is to give each actor their undivided attention. This will encourage each person to give their very best to convince the team they should be cast.

Through all of this, the musical director needs to be hearing and seeing these people in light of the upcoming production, thinking how their singing fits into the overall plan for the production. Give everyone your full attention, and make them feel that you have been waiting all day for the chance to observe their audition!

One very important element of the entire audition procedure should not be omitted. Never allow the person to sing their audition without musical accompaniment. Unaccompanied singing tells you nothing about how well or poorly they sing with accompaniment, nor anything of their rhythmic ability and accuracy of pitch. One writer further emphasizes this point by stating, "It is extraordinarily difficult to stay on pitch without the aid of a musical instrument and it is extremely awkward-sounding" (Oliver 47). If someone appears at an audition without a prepared piece of music to sing, or without a copy of the music to give to the accompanist, that person is not only being unprofessional, but also is being naïve. Oliver concludes with a message to these actors: "You might as well have stayed at home" (Oliver 47).

If you are in a position to advise students or people in the community on proper audition etiquette, you could give them some advice on the choice of material to sing for the audition. If they wish to be considered for a particular part, a selection that character sings would be appropriate to perform. But the best advice, is to remind the actor that they *must* bring their own music to the audition. That it should be legible, the pages in the correct order, and the music is in the key the actor wishes to sing it goes without question (Oliver 47). Never show up unprepared.

And, this brings us to the most important person at any audition: the *autition accompanist*. Ideally, an accompanist is provided at the audition and this information is included in the audition announcement. The rehearsal/audition accompanist person should be considered as part of the production staff. This person could be the same person who will serve as the rehearsal accompanist. Regardless of who it is, they must be an excellent sight-reader and be extremely alert to the needs of each singer. During the audition times, the accompanist will have to play a variety of musical selections in different musical styles for a number of actors. When you have a good rehearsal/audition accompanist available, treat this person with respect, because the success and failure of an actor's audition is often in their hands.

In amateur or college auditions, it is acceptable for each person to bring their own accompanist if they are more comfortable working with a particular person. Some people have auditioned quite successfully by bringing a tape player with a taped accompaniment of their selection. This works fine, too. At no time, however, should the musical director be the accompanist for any of the auditions. By sitting at the keyboard and playing for an audition, it is almost impossible to listen fairly and accurately, much less be able to see their facial expressions.

Professional accompanists are a breed unto themselves. A few years ago, I was in New York City on an audition trip and a professional accompanist had been hired. Because of the ability of these talented people, I was sometimes more impressed by their playing than by the actors I heard singing. One incident is particularly memorable. When a nervous actor began to go sharp and sing a half-step higher, the alert accompanist modulated instantly with him and played the song in the new key to the end. "I didn't plan to modulate," said the actor at the end of the song. "But you did," replied the accompanist. No wonder these talented people are well paid and are able make their living at this job!

Chapter 5

Call-Backs

Let us pretend you heard about eighty people sing their best sixteen to twenty-four measures of music at the auditions and you have seen these eighty people learn and perform some type of dance combination. If monologs were required, these have been heard as well. The director, the choreographer, and the musical director will then meet to prepare the list of people needed to appear at the next step in the audition process, call-backs. If you have kept accurate notes during the auditions, you will be able to speak confidently at this meeting. The director is in charge of this meeting and expects comments, observations and opinions from you and the choreographer. The musical director should indicate how large a chorus he thinks he will need. With the people who auditioned, will it be possible to achieve the correct balance of men and women needed to sing the music?

The list of names can be dealt with in several ways. One way would be to eliminate the people that you think are not correct for the show, either because of vocal reasons, or due to movement ability, age, size, or whatever. The director will look through the list and suggest the names he would like to hear read for certain principal roles. Your comments on their vocal abilities will support or negate his decision. The director will have in mind the people who seem right for the smaller roles, or "bit-parts." For call-backs, it is best that there be at least two people to consider for each of the principal roles. This will allow you to compare the musical performances of each at the call-back time. This also assures that no single person is automatically given a part. It also keeps an element of suspense and competition in the air as to whom will be cast!

The call-back period will be the best time to have the actors sing selections from the show. When call-backs are announced, giving the names of the people that the team wishes to hear sing/read, it is your job to indicate what music you wish each person to perform. Since your responsibility deals with the vocalist's abilities, you will want to select passages that are the most difficult and challenging for the actor to sing. If the role requires the actor to sing a ballad, this is when you discover if they have the lyrical singing style required to negotiate the ballad number in the show. Or, if the role calls for a high B-flat, you can be sure that everyone auditioning for that part needs to prove that they have or do not have the high B-flat required. You will want to avoid the incident that occurred in a high school production of *The King and I* where the student cast as Tuptim had difficulty with the high notes in her solos throughout the rehearsal period. Things were not improving, so the student took it upon herself to solve the situation and at the last dress rehearsal began taking all the high notes down an octave but singing the rest of the number at pitch. While satisfying the problem of singing pitches out of her range, it considerably altered the composer's intention.

Therefore, if you are doing *Annie Get Your Gun,* you might ask all the men being considered for the role of Frank Butler to sing "The Girl That I Marry" in addition to any other material you wish to hear. At the call-back time, ask the men who are auditioning for "Frank" to come forward and sing as a group the required song or portion of the song you have indicated for them to prepare. That way you can be sure they all learned the correct portion of the music and know the correct tempo. You can listen for note accuracy as they sing together. This procedure will give the novice actor some confidence as he sings the song in a group before having to perform it as a solo. When you are confident that they all know the music well enough to sing it alone, ask each person to sing individually what they have just sung all together. Rate each of them on some sort of scale similar to what you used during the audition times. As they perform, notice how well prepared they are, or how quickly they learned the music, as well as the quality of their voice. The most important observation will be to observe if they can sing as the character they are to portray. When each person sings, be sure you sit on the other side of the room, or out in the auditorium, so you will have a better perspective of the sound, projection, and character portrayal. You can use the same procedure for duets—rehearse first as a group, then have the same music sung in different pairs. You can hear how the voices blend, and notice if one voice is more powerful than the other. You can also observe how they relate as a couple. At no time during this procedure should you serve as the audition pianist!

As you listen, you might be able to determine if the person has learned the work from the recording or on their own. Will they be flexible enough to accept your directions, or is the song already firmly implanted in their mind and what you are hearing is all that you will ever get? During the first audition step, it is not appropriate for the musical director to ask the actor to repeat a portion of his song. At that time you are just hearing people. The call-back time is different. It is completely permissible for you to ask the actor to repeat a selection asking that it be sung softer or louder, faster or slower, to sing it more freely or more rhythmically. Or, you could just indicate that you would like to hear it sung differently. This might give you a feel for the actor's flexibility and if they can take direction. This procedure happens all the time at auditions for plays. The director could ask an actor to repeat the prepared monolog with a totally different approach than what had just been delivered.

In addition to hearing musical selections sung at call-backs, the director will have various combinations of actors read portions of scenes from the script. This will be done in pairs or small groups, depending upon the chosen scene. These group readings will be done until all the actors have all had a chance to read for the character for which they are being considered. The director could even ask for the actors to do some improvisation, further showing their acting skills. At call-backs, it may even be necessary for the choreographer to have people dance again. And you may need to have your ears refreshed by asking for another rendition by any singer of a particular musical selection. At the end of call-backs, the director, the choreographer, and the musical director meet together to make the final casting decisions. But, the final decision for casting is the director's responsibility, aided by your input.

Auditions and Call-Backs for Children

Many shows have roles for children. You can not very well do *The Sound of Music*, or *The King and I* without children of a variety of ages. Some musicals, such as *Oliver!* and *Annie* require a child to be capable of playing a leading role. Sometimes, auditions for young people can be difficult because the child will be overcome with fright when asked to sing in front of strangers and will barely be able to make an audible sound. Or a child may be auditioning only because their parents are insisting that they do this, when being on stage is the last thing he wants to do. Other children can be quite insistent about auditioning and urge their parents to set up a time for them. Then, they will freeze when they need to sing or read in front of the directing team. The purpose of the audition, however, is the same for children as it is for adults: you need to find out what they are able to do!

It is preferable to audition children at a separate time from the adult cast members. For their audition, the children should come prepared to sing a song they know. Sometimes it is a Christmas carol; sometimes it is a song they learned in school, or in church. Children should sing with accompaniment just as the adult actors do, but this is not always possible, as they may not have access to the musical scores they want to sing. In these cases, give them a starting pitch, or just let them pick a note out of the air to sing their selection. Many times boys want to sound mature and will try and pitch the song very low, when what you want to hear is their unchanged voice.

Very young children may not be good readers. Instead of having them read from a script, they could be asked to recite a poem from memory. The writings of Shel Silverstein, Lois Duncan, and Jack Prelutsky are favorites with youngsters because of the subject matter and the rhythm pattern of the verse. After they have recited and sung their prepared selections individually, have a group of the children learn a short passage of music they will sing in the show. Learning in a group usually saves time, and gives confidence to those who are a little shy. Copies of the song are passed out for those who can read either words or music; the others learn by rote. Then, after the music has been learned, each child is asked to sing individually what they have just been taught as a group. In this way you can see how quickly they can pick up music, and if they are able to hold a part should harmony be required. When doing this type of audition, I always allow the child who sang first to sing again after the last child has sung. I feel the others had an advantage of hearing the others sing that he did not have.

Finally, the director will have the children read a scene from the show in pairs or combinations, or read a scene with an adult who might be playing a part in the show. When a child is right physically for a part, but stumbles too much over the text another tactic may be used to see if they can create a character. The child is asked to mime such tasks as taking a shirt out of the closet, put it on, and walk out of the house; or, mime making a bed; or, get the right ingredients out of the cabinet in order to make a peanut-butter sandwich! These little mime exercises are wonderful ways to see if children can project an idea and move without inhibition.

The goals of the musical director will be the same in hearing children's auditions as in hearing other auditions. You will be listening for the size of the child's voice, their pitch, clarity of diction, as well as if they are the right voice type for the part. The director will make the final decision depending upon which children fit into his concept for the production, but your comments regarding their musical abilities are crucial in this decision-making process.

Chapter 6

Casting

After the time for the auditions and call-backs has taken place, the final decision has to be made. This may be done by the director alone, or by the team. Your comments will be a part of the total decision process. Be sure to state whom you prefer and why. Ideally, one casts the person who is the best actor-singer-dancer. Rarely, especially in amateur productions, will you find all three of these areas to be of equal strength in the same person. Often, excellent singers cannot act; excellent dancers cannot sing; excellent actors cannot move or sing. Miller comments about this problem with high school students, but his observations are pertinent to any level of theatrical production.

> Too often a person is cast in musicals because of the quality of his voice, without paying proper attention to his ability to act. Both are essential. No musical should be attempted . . . unless you have high school students who can sing well, interpret roles superbly, and have the talent for the characterizations that are called for. Songs must be interpreted just as parts are, and the actor must remain in character while he is singing. (L. Miller 32)

However, after making that observation by Miller, it will be noted that when undertaking any production that requires emphasis upon good singing, such as Sondheim's *A Little Night Music,* the actor must have an excellent singing voice to begin with. One writer suggests "The director can usually 'teach' a singer how to act, or an actor how to act more competently" (Hustoles 183). The director will be more successful in evoking some suggestion of emotional interpretation out of an amateur actor over a short period of time than the musical director will be in getting a person to learn to sing "unless the actor already possesses the necessary (vocal) skills" (Hustoles 183).

At the auditions and call-backs, one had the opportunity to test all of these areas. During the casting meeting one tries to put the pieces of the puzzle together and come up with the best combination of people to fill the parts in the show. Some compromises must be made when there does not seem to be a clear cut winner with all of the right qualities for the character being cast. One must try and look ahead to see if a person can grow into a part, or can expand their acting or singing or dancing abilities to be able to fulfill the requirements for the part. However, often the audition process is a good example of "what you see is what you get." Casting is never an easy task. But, through the audition and the call-back process, with the careful notes and observations that have been made, the directing team will cast the show. A group of people will be assembled to make up the cast and with whom you will be working in an intense relationship on a regular basis for the coming weeks.

Some high school directors have noticed that the type of student who auditions for a show is also involved in a number of school activities. Will they be able to adjust their schedules to devote the required amount of time to rehearsals and performances? One of the biggest rehearsal conflicts is with athletic schedules. Coaches are as demanding about practice time as directors are for rehearsals. Would a student be willing to work around conflicts? You don't want your leading man missing a performance because of a championship ball game. In some schools, students have auditioned and been cast in musical theatre productions even though it has meant discontinuing participation in an athletic activity. They understood there was no way they could take part in both.

At last! The huge, first hurdle has been successfully conquered. Schedule conflicts have been resolved. The cast-list is ready to be posted and the first rehearsal is scheduled. The task of molding and shaping the members of the cast into characters is about to begin. The job of transferring the printed word of script and music into live action and sound is ready to start. And, at long last, the true work of the musical director begins.

Chapter 7

Chorus Books/Vocal Parts

The musical director will rehearse and conduct from the piano/vocal score. This is the published, engraved score, which can be purchased in a music store which contains all the music for the show. However, the scores for many musicals are not available for purchase and can only be rented. This rented material can be printed or written by hand.

The cast members will not be working from the piano/vocal score. They have a different situation. Some publishers print booklets with the full script of the show located in the front and all the vocal music for the show located in the back all bound in the same volume. Even though the text of the songs is in the script, the actors will need to shift to the back of the book for the music with the text. There are shows when the cast is required to juggle two books: one that contains the script and a separate chorus book, which contains all the show's music. The music book is called the chorus book or vocal parts book, because it contains all the music of the show that is sung by principals as well as chorus. Even when dialog and music are in the same volume, it is commonly referred to as a script.

In some cases, the script is chopped up into little booklets known as "sides." A side contains all the lines that an individual character speaks in the show, with cue lines just before each speech. For example, Mr. Brownlow in *Oliver* would have a side containing all of Brownlow's lines. Just prior to each of Brownlow's speeches, there is a cue line of the actor who speaks just before him. Not all publishers use sides, but, Tams Witmark, for example, will "often send sides instead of full scripts for the performers. A side consists of the cues and lines for a particular performer or character, deleting the lines of all other characters" (Laughlin and Wheeler 5). In the side, there is no indication as to who says the speech immediately preceding the one to be spoken, or how much conversation has taken place between speeches. It is only at the first read-through of the script, or by looking at the full script, that the actor knows how many other conversations appear between his speeches. This sounds terribly confusing, but it is amazing how quickly one adjusts to the situation.

Perhaps an example of dialog from a fictitious musical will illustrate this more clearly. Here is a page from the script showing all the dialog.

MARY: *(innocently)* What time do you think we will be able to leave for the beach?
BOB: Not sure. It depends how long it takes to change the spark plugs.
JOE But, I want to leave now!
MARY: *(exasperated)* You can't even give me an approximate time?
BOB: No, honey. At least a couple of hours.
JOE: But, if we don't get there soon, I'll miss all the fun.
BOB: Come on, Joe. Give me a break!
JOE: Didn't you say you'd get this done yesterday so we could leave early?
BOB: Yeah, but something came up.
JOE: What?
BOB: Something.
JOE: What?
MARY: *(frustrated)* Can't you give him an answer, Bob?

Example 7-1. Page from Script of *Beach Journey*

Notice that in Example 7-2, Mary has only her part and a cue line. She does not know that the word "What" is said two times before she says her next line. Is it any wonder actors prefer to use scripts?

MARY: *(innocently)* What time do you think we will be able to leave for the beach?
... want to leave now!
MARY: *(exasperated)* You can't even give me an approximate time?
... What?
MARY: *(frustrated)* Can't you give him an answer, Bob?

Example 7-2.
Page from the Side for the Character Mary from *Beach Journey*

Just as the piano/vocal score can be either handwritten or engraved, the same situation exists for the music parts for principals and chorus. The chorus/ vocal books contain only the melody line with lyrics written below the music. None of the accompaniment is shown. The music for men as well as women is written in treble clef. Obviously, the men should sing an octave lower than what is written. In most cases, the bass clef is used only when the chorus is broken into an open choral score format with each part having their own vocal line (see Example 7-3). Closed score (like hymn-book notation) is frequently used as well.

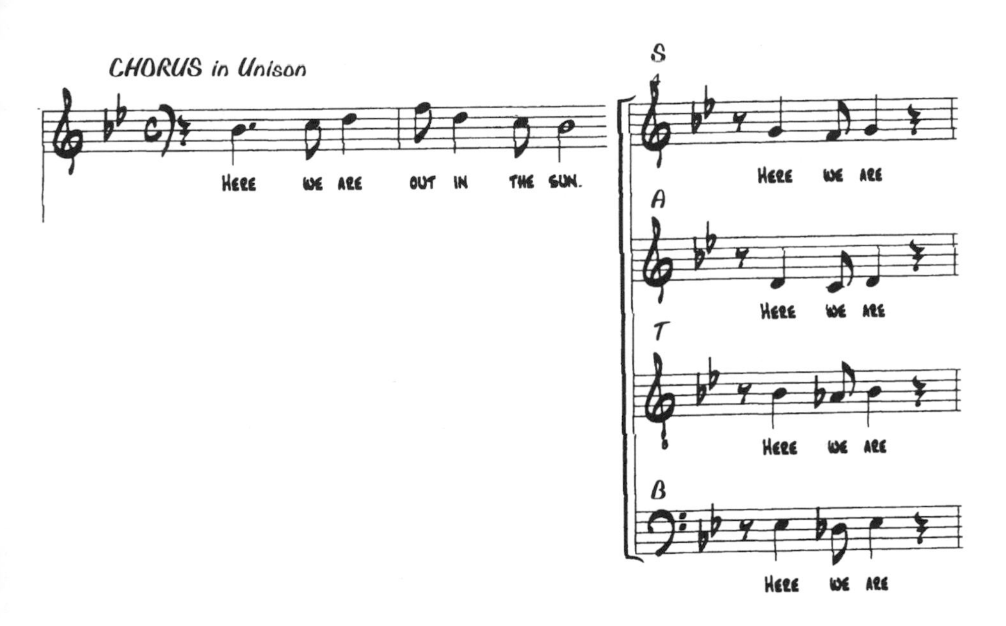

Example 7-3.
"Out in the Sun" from *Beach Journey*

If there are places in the chorus for a principal to sing alone or with another character, these parts will be indicated, again without showing any of the accompaniment (see Example 7-4).

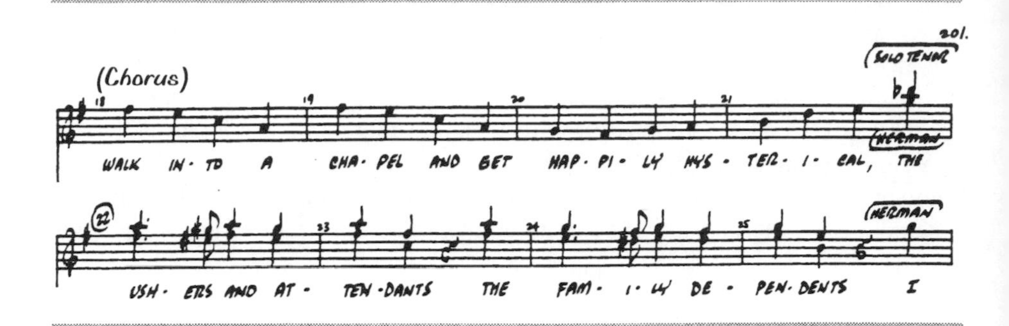

Example 7-4. "I Love to Cry at Weddings" from *Sweet Charity* *(used by permission)*

Sometimes it is not always clear in which octave a singer is to sing. In the example shown below, the entire chorus is to sing in unison the pitch "e-1" (E above middle C). When first looking at the music, it appears that the women are to sing "e-2" and the men to sing "e-1." The note in the score, "Girls sing 8-Bassa unison w/men," clarifies the pitch level that is to be sung. In this case, the women would sing an octave lower than written, thus singing in unison with the men (see Example 7-5).

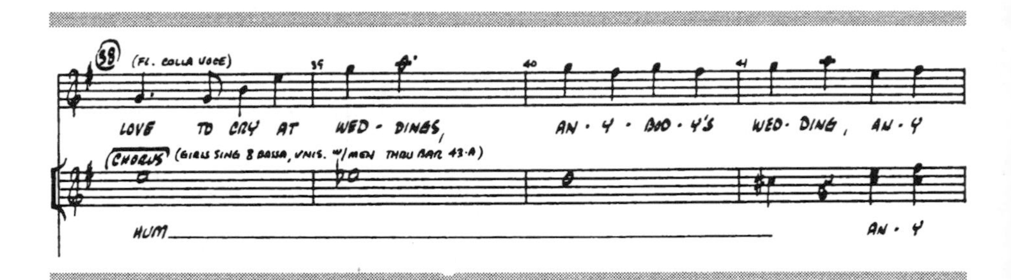

Example 7-5. "I Love to Cry at Weddings" from *Sweet Charity* *(used by permission)*

Chorus books vary in accuracy and clarity. It is not uncommon for there to be discrepancies in text as well as musical notation between the chorus/vocal books and the piano/vocal score. Errors can occur in both in the engraved and the handwritten versions. The musical director will need to determine which text or notes are correct and indicate this to the actors. Usually, the variation in text can be solved by consulting the full-text version of the script. It will be worth your while to take the time to compare a copy of a chorus book with the piano/vocal score. Also, be prepared to have the cast members ask questions!

Chapter 8

First Music Rehearsal with Cast

Schedule

The final decision has been made. The cast list is posted. The tears of joy and groans of disappointment are over. You are ready to get started. At the beginning of the rehearsal time when learning the music is the top priority, the musical director is in charge of the rehearsal schedule as well as deciding what actors are needed and when. Once the music has been learned and scene work begins, the director is in charge of deciding which items are to be worked on at each rehearsal. In both cases, the stage manager will post this information for all to see.

Traditionally, the first rehearsal is a time when all the cast members assemble for the reading of the script. It is a good way for everyone to hear the entire script and have an idea of what the show is about. At this meeting the director will give the ground rules for the production: attendance requirements, rehearsal dates, costume fitting appointments, performance dates, and other information. The scripts are distributed and then read with each member taking his assigned part. Where musical items occur, they are either skipped, or a recording of the music is played.

Some first rehearsals are "table rehearsals" where the actors sit around a table and read the script, getting a feel for the text and how they relate with each other. This works best, I think, for straight plays rather than musicals. Some directors dispense with a group reading of the script and dive right into blocking the show at the first rehearsal. If the latter is the case, an actor who is in only one scene at the end of Act II will never know how his scene fits into the overall scheme of the show until time for run throughs! But some directors prefer to work that way and that is their privilege.

Another way to begin the show's first rehearsal, which seems to get everyone involved very quickly, is to rehearse the musical numbers prior to the first read-through. These music rehearsals could take a couple of weeks of daily rehearsals. Or, these could be two or three sessions of two hours each. The amount of time required to learn the music will vary according to the amount of rehearsal time as well as the abilities of the cast. When the music is thoroughly learned, there will be a "read/sing through" of the show. If the organizational meeting did not take place prior to the first music rehearsal, the read/sing rehearsal will be the best time to have it. At the read/sing through everyone reads their assigned roles and the principals and chorus sing all the music they have already learned. Naturally, the dance routines or special numbers are eliminated. I prefer having the music rehearsals first, as it involves the majority of the cast members from the very first reading.

Planning for Music Rehearsals

If the music rehearsals take place first, it is crucial that you plan for these efficiently. If this is a community production, remember that the cast members are volunteers, so it is your responsibility as musical director to use their time well. If they are students, they will have other things to do when not on call for a rehearsal, such as classes or homework, so they will still appreciate your good use of the rehearsal time. With professionals, it is a little different, as they are probably under contract to the production and are able to devote their full attention to rehearsals with few outside conflicts. Still efficient use of rehearsal time is always appreciated regardless of the situation.

To begin a rehearsal with the first number of the show, then go to the second number, rehearsing through the score to the very end, is not a good use of the cast's time. If you rehearsed in this manner, you might have a room full of people waiting to sing a number that appears at the end of Act I while you spend time rehearsing music for the people that appear earlier! One suggestion for an expedient use of the cast's time is to rehearse the music by grouping people together for their numbers regardless of where these selections appear in the show. For example, rehearse all the numbers using the full chorus first. The chorus could even be rehearsed with men and women separately. Then, shift to the numbers involving only a trio or a quartet or a smaller group of singers. Finally, rehearse the solos and duets.

Let's pretend you are the musical director for *Damn Yankees* by Richard Adler and Jerry Ross. The score lists the musical items which call for soloists and/or chorus as shown in Example 8-1.

Act I	#2 – Six Months Out of Every Year (Meg, Joe, Men, Women)
	#4 – Goodbye, Old Girl (Old Joe, Young Joe)
	#5 – Heart (VanBuren, Rocky, Vernon, Smokey)
	#6 – Heart (Reprise)
	#7 – Shoeless Joe from Hannibal, Mo (Gloria, Ballplayers)
	#10 – A Man Doesn't Know (Young Joe)
	#12 – A Little Brains, A Little Talent (Lola)
	#13 – Goodbye, Old Girl (Reprise) (Young Joe)
	#14 – A Man Doesn't Know (Reprise) (Young Joe, Meg)
	#15 – Whatever Lola Wants (Lola)
	#17 – Heart (Reprise) (Sister, Fan Club)
	#19 – Who's Got the Pain? (Lola, Eddie)
Act II	#24 – The Game (Rocky, Smokey, Mickey, Lowe, Henry & Ballplayers)
	#25 – Near to You (Young Joe, Meg)
	#26 – Those Were the Good Old Days (Applegate)
	#27 – Those Were the Good Old Days (Reprise) (Applegate)
	#28 – Two Lost Souls (Lola, Young Joe)
	#32 – A Man Doesn't Know (Reprise) (Old Joe, Meg)
	#33 – Heart (Reprise)

Example 8-1. Musical Items for Soloists and/or Chorus

The numbers not listed are for the orchestra, such as scene change music, overture, etc. If the rehearsal began with the first number and ran from the first piece of music to the closing number, the chorus would only be involved in singing items #2 and #33. This is hardly a good use of rehearsal time.

Selecting numbers which use the same people and rehearsing these together in groups would produce a schedule that might look like Example 8-2.

7:00–7:15	Applegate	#26 & #27 – Those Were the Good Old Days and Reprise
7:15–7:45	Lola	#23 – A Little Brains a Little Talent #15 – Whatever Lola Wants #19 – Who's Got the Pain (with Eddie) #28 – Two Lost Souls (with Young Joe)
7:45–8:10	Young Joe & Meg	#10 & #14 – A Man Doesn't Know #25 – Near To You #13 – Goodbye Old Girl
8:10–8:35	Old Joe & Meg	#32 – A Man Doesn't Know # 4 – Goodbye Old Girl # 2 – Six Months Out of Every Year (no chorus)
8:35–8:45	Full Cast	#33 – Heart
8:45–9:10	Chorus, Meg, Old Joe	# 6 – Six Months Out of Every Year
9:10–9:15	Sister, Fan Club	#17 – Heart (Reprise)
9:15–9:40	Gloria, Chorus Men	# 8 – Shoeless Joe from Hannibal, Mo
9:40–10:10	Male Chorus	#24 – The Game
10:10–10:30	VanBuren, Rocky, Vernon, Smokey	#5 & #6 – Heart

Example 8-2. Sample Rehearsal Schedule

This suggested schedule organizes the numbers into blocks, trying as much as possible to use the cast for numbers that they sing so that they have as little down-time as possible. The evening's rehearsal begins at 7:00 p.m. with Applegate's solo, "Those Were the Good Old Days." After Applegate's solo has been rehearsed, it does mean that the actor playing Applegate will have to wait until 8:35 through the closing number. During this wait he could work on his lines or read a good book!

Lola's numbers are either solos, duets, or dances. The block of time from 7:15–7:45 uses only three people: Lola and the two people who sing with her, Young Joe and Eddie. The next two rehearsal blocks use Meg with Young Joe and Old Joe. While they are rehearsing, Lola can either take a break or work on her lines with Applegate. The full cast has been called for 8:35 to learn the closing number of the show which is short and easy. It should not take too much time to learn this song. At 8:45, Applegate and Lola are finished for the evening.

Old Joe and Meg have already rehearsed their parts in the show's opening number, "Six Months Out of Every Year." The 8:45–9:10 time block is for the chorus to learn their parts of this number. Since Meg and Old Joe are called for the same time block, the number can be run with everyone involved. After this has been completed, the female chorus members may be dismissed except for those who have been cast as members of the Fan Club and sing number #17, the reprise of "Heart." This reprise can be worked out in a very short time. The next two time blocks use the men of the chorus along with Gloria for "Shoeless Joe." At 10:10, the only people needed are the four actors who sing "Heart" bringing the music rehearsal to a close.

This rehearsal plan can work just as easily in reverse order, e.g. starting with the full cast and then subtracting people until you are working with small groups or individuals. The amount of time needed for learning music depends upon the group's abilities and will thus vary. The intention of this schedule was to rehearse music for the entire show within a two and a half hour time block. Working in this manner means that the musical director and the rehearsal accompanist are on duty for the entire time period, but there is no way around that. It also means that the rehearsal should move at a pretty fast pace. The advantage to working in this manner is that it uses the cast's time in the most efficient manner possible. It does not take into consideration working with understudies. If understudies are used, they should appear at the time block when the principals are called, as well as at the chorus times. Depending upon your situation, you may need more or less time than suggested to learn the music. Music rehearsals could be held over a period of several evenings depending on the time allowed in the production schedule by the director.

Dividing the chorus by gender is another way for learning notes. For shows that have a number of items for the chorus, first call the men (tenors and basses) from 7:00–8:30, and then from 8:30–10:00 rehearse the same music with the women (sopranos and altos). By breaking the chorus into two groups, part learning goes faster. It also seems to be a good use of time. For example, while you were making sure the altos had their part, only one group, the sopranos, would be waiting, rather than three voice groups being idle while one part is being rehearsed. This method would work efficiently at any place in the score where part-singing takes place, whether it be small or large groupings. Once each section was secure with its part, put the men's and women's sections together. In these part/note learning rehearsals, the accompanist will play only the voice parts, but later add either the missing voice parts or a sparse accompaniment. Learning notes in this manner will work quite successfully with those who do not read music, but learn by rote. Later, when a rehearsal for the full chorus is called, everyone will be able to sing together fairly securely.

I have seen the use of gender divided rehearsals work in both professional and amateur production, and observed that it was a successful approach in both situations. It also works well when the music reading skills of the chorus are weak. The more traditional way of having all the chorus rehearse together can be equally successful. Regardless of which you use, the result is the same: you are teaching notes and training the chorus singers for their part in the production.

As musical director, you may find that making tapes for the singers will be a way of reinforcing your work outside of the scheduled rehearsal time. Many church choir directors have used this method successfully, and it can work equally well in theatrical rehearsals. These tapes do not have to be of the best quality, but they do need to be accurate as to pitches and rhythm. If you feel comfortable using your own voice and playing the part on the piano to make these tapes, then do so. If you prefer not to have your voice present on a tape, use a student or another member of the cast to assist you in making the rehearsal tapes. The rehearsal tape allows the actor to listen/practice on his own outside of rehearsal time. Rehearsal tapes are equally valuable for principals as well as chorus members. This is especially helpful for people who do not have a piano and wish to practice their parts on their own. I have observed the successful use of rehearsal tapes in both professional and amateur productions.

During the early music rehearsals, the musical director will find it an absolute must to use the rehearsal time efficiently and work very fast. There is a lot to learn and, frequently, not too much time. Plus there are tons of minute details to be ironed out. As the musical director, you should be able to indicate clearly what you want and to rehearse in such a way that you obtain the desired result. Even in rehearsal you should strive to work for a high energy level from the chorus that is vital and contagious. It helps if the conductor is able to convey this same energy as well, as it will transfer to the cast. The reason for working in this manner is because the next activity for the cast members will be the blocking of scenes under the leadership of the director, or they may be receiving movement instructions from the choreographer. During these times, all their concentration will be on their movement and action rather than singing. Therefore, the music must be learned prior to these activities so that the cast can concentrate on these other tasks.

Regardless of how you decide to use your music rehearsal time, you will need to post the schedule for the cast where everyone can see indicating the times when people should appear in a location. This might be on the bulletin board outside your classroom or near the theatre's rehearsal space. You might warn the cast that the posted times are approximate, as you might spend a little more time than planned on certain numbers due to unforeseen problems. Insist that people appear early just in case the opposite takes place and you get ahead of your planned schedule.

If you have a week to learn the music for the show, you could post a daily rehearsal schedule. Or better yet, post a schedule for the entire music rehearsal period. If your cast has email access, the schedule can be distributed electronically. Even if you make last minute changes, they can be notified quickly, provided the cast checks their email. For the first rehearsal periods, most of the time will be devoted to learning the notes. Some productions allow a week's time, rehearsing three to four times a week, to get all the music learned. Later music rehearsals will be more of a run through paying attention to note accuracy, tempo, rhythm, dynamics, and diction. Once the music is learned, the director will post the rehearsal schedule indicating which scenes are to be blocked and rehearsed with the approximate times cast members are to appear. This schedule can be printed and distributed to each cast member as well as posted in some convenient location. A schedule of this type is especially helpful in community groups when one must plan rehearsal times around work obligations. Again, email can be very helpful.

Vocal Technique

Time is a crucial rehearsal factor. In addition to teaching the music to the cast members, the musical director will be concerned with other musical matters from the very first rehearsal. Insist on accurate attacks and releases at all times. Do not accept any variation in note accuracy. Work to achieve the tone you want from the chorus by beginning with vocal warm-ups as well as throughout the note-learning process. The tone needs to vary from the full-voiced, chest-quality sound so typical of Broadway shows, to the use of the head voice or with a mix of the two in the middle register. Listen carefully to determine if the chest voice is being carried too high, especially by the female singers. After the notes have been learned and you are running the music, encourage everyone to use their voices exactly the same way in rehearsal that they will use it in performance.

During the note-learning process, there is no need for the chorus to sing full voice for the entire rehearsal. However, it has been my experience that some singers will object at the mere suggestion of singing softly and insist on singing full voice even when notes are being pounded out. They seem to feel it is their duty to show you what strong singers they are. A lot of vocal energy will be wasted if you permit the chorus to sing loudly during the note-learning time. Lighter singing allows them hear what is taking place around them and how their part fits in with the others. It will take stern discipline to get this idea across. In addition, encourage the actors to save their voices while learning choreography or going through what seems like endless repetitions of the same scene. This will assure healthy voices at performance time.

Singing softly does not mean singing with no energy, nor does it mean casual or careless singing. Since the early rehearsal time is the note-learning period, loud singing is a waste of time and vocal energy. In subsequent rehearsals, once the notes have been learned, allow them to sing at the required dynamic level. As mentioned earlier, the chorus will probably reject the idea of singing softly while learning notes as most will want to sing the music at the top of their lungs.

Soft, rhythmic, energetic singing has an effective use in performance. One of the most exciting choruses in all of musical theatre is the "Ascot Gavotte" from *My Fair Lady*. This number, where "the upper classes sing a satire about themselves" (Hustoles 158) is successful only when every member of the ensemble is aware of the careful and crisp articulation of both text and notes that is required. If one person does not put space between the syllables, it comes out muddy. If the tempo is not perfectly rigid, it will rush. If it is sung too loudly, it loses its appeal. All of these musical errors destroy the haughty demeanor the chorus is trying to portray in the scene. It takes exacting rehearsal and careful attention to detail to make this chorus, as well as the entire repertoire of the show, sound correct. Full-voiced singing would destroy this delicate number.

Require the chorus to know the number of beats long notes are held, especially in final chords. This will assure good, precise releases even without a cut-off gesture from the conductor. Insist from the very beginning that phrasing be the same throughout. Urge the singers to memorize quickly. This means not just memorizing the notes and words, but knowing on what beat the final consonant will fall, the color of vowels, or the use of dialect, if required.

In addition to learning notes, number of beats notes are held, and where consonants fall, the musical director will need to listen for correct vowels sung by all cast members. This is an area of prime concern for choral directors who devote a great deal of time in choral rehearsals for vowel unification by the ensemble. Yet too much vowel unity in the theatre ensemble will detract, making it sound too much like a choir. However, attention to vowels is too often a neglected area which can affect the overall production. I recall attending a performance where the male lead sang the words "To" and "You" with a distorted vowel sound on particular words. For example, the preposition "To" was pronounced "Tew" and the pronoun "You" came out as "Ewe." Therefore, the phrase, "I love you" was rendered as "I love ewe." (Could he have been singing to a sheep?) This distorted pronunciation was so blatant that it destroyed any beauty in the ballad he sang.

In some way, one can understand why this happened. One hears this vowel being mispronounced more and more in spoken language. One has only to listen to television and radio announcers to notice it. Therefore, it is no wonder it creeps into singing. The other reason, is that the "ooh" vowel is more dark and covered while the "ewe" sound is more forward and brighter. The singer may have felt more comfortable with the latter as it carries better. In the production I attended, the singer needed to modify the vowel to avoid sounding comical! An alert musical director could have prevented the singer from falling into this trap.

In working with the actor/singers, it may be necessary to help them with good vocal production. I may be wrong, but I feel that good singing is good singing, regardless of where it takes place, whether it be in a choral ensemble, in a church choir, on stage, an operatic aria, or a simple ballad. The requirements of right notes, right rhythms, right vowels, and right dynamics, combined with proper breath support and correct intonation remain the same! The haunting beauty of the choral opening of *Brigadoon* requires the same attention to vocal tuning as a choir singing a Brahms motet. The "Tonight Quintet" (known as "Tonight" in the score and sometimes called the "Tonight Montage") from *West Side Story,* requires good musicianship as well as good vocal singing to bring off the contrapuntal complexity of this exciting number! Your job as musical director is to make sure that the singing is in tune and with correct rhythm (just as one would expect for any type of vocal music!), that words can be understood, and that the style is appropriate to the show.

You will want to be alerted to two other vocal concerns: the use of vibrato and chest voice. Excessive vibrato is frequently a problem with older singers, particularly in women. Sometimes this results from a lack of support, or by pushing the voice too much. Or it could come from a severe case of nerves. Another vocal concern is the use of the chest voice, especially by women. If the chest voice is carried too high, not only will the sound be unpleasant, but the singer is often times endangering her own vocal health. She may be able to make it through the rehearsal period, with the understudy having to step in and perform the part in the actual performance. Helping young singers learn to mix registers is time consuming. In a college/university setting, the actor/singer can take the music to his studio voice teacher for additional help. In the professional world, they will seek out the help of a professional vocal coach. It is in the high school and amateur production that the musical director may find that he has the added responsibility of vocal teacher/vocal coach added to his list of duties.

The musical director will want to be alert to a practice that sometimes develops in productions after the show is blocked. This is the habit of some actors to alter the notes on the page and begin to embellish them. The most offensive is that of singing behind the beat, then rushing notes together to catch up. This is sometimes referred to as back-phrasing. "It is often a result of over-indulgence on the part of the performer, and it an affectation which needs to be closely monitored by the musical director. Back-phrasing can be an effective means of expression, but when used indiscriminately, it can be extremely irritating" (White 73). On the other hand, it is an excellent musical device in expressing feeling in a song allowing the singer to "bend" the phrase or to place emphasis on certain words. However, if it is incorporated too frequently it will destroy the composer's original intention. Therefore, it needs careful attention by both the actor and the musical director.

Chapter 9

Style

For the musical director style is a pertinent topic for both singers and instrumentalists. The director will probably talk with the cast early in the rehearsal period about his concept of style for the show. He will try to give the actors a feeling for the show, a time period, and some background information they can use to create the characters they are to portray. He may share historical material regarding the time period in which the show is set. The style for *Fiddler on the Roof* is certainly different than the style of *The Boy Friend.* The costume designer will accent this sense of style in the way the cast is dressed. The set designer will try and create a comparable visual setting for the action to take place. The choreographer will take the director's choice of style and incorporate this in the movement that is to be taught.

Understanding musical style is equally important. But, how does one learn about it, and more importantly, how does one teach this concept or get the idea across to the cast during the rehearsal period? It is essential for a musical director to listen to as many recordings as possible of different Broadway productions. It is even beneficial to hear different recordings, if available, of the same show, especially if a film version of the show has been made. If the opportunity avails itself, the musical director will want to attend as many live musical productions as possible. This will not only provide an enjoyable evening on the town, but it will serve as an opportunity to expands one's ears and eyes by observing how things are done in the professional world. By taking every opportunity to broaden your own knowledge, you will find that you will be able to share these experiences with the people with whom you are working.

There are a number of musical theatre styles. There is a flapper and collegiate style of the 1920s, there is a Rodgers and Hammerstein style of lyrical singing, there is a style for the works of Steven Sondheim. There is obviously a style for doing music of the 1960s as in the musical, *Grease,* just as there is the *Les Mis* style of singing in the works of Boublil and Schönberg. It would be incorrect to sing in a *Les Mis* style when performing *Oklahoma* and the reverse would be equally true. Serious theatre students tend to pick up on these variations of style because they do a great deal of listening to recordings of various productions.

Many shows require the use of dialect in the singing. Although not indicated in the score, it is customary for the men to use a French accent when singing "Canaan Days" in *Joseph and the Amazing Technicolor Dreamcoat.* This certainly adds to the effectiveness and is the correct style for that song. It will be the duty of the musical director to see that a song is sung with the correct accent. When accents or dialects are required in the spoken part of the show, the director will provide the correct guide to pronunciation, but in the sung portions this is the musical director's responsibility.

In shows such as *Joseph and the Amazing Technicolor Dreamcoat,* or *Children of Eden,* it will be obvious that in many of the selections for solo voice, there is a great deal of variation between what the singer does on the original cast recording (sometimes called the Broadway cast recording or album) and what appears on the printed page of music. And your cast may have learned the music by listening to these recordings. What do you do? Do you ask the singer to learn the notes as they appear, or imitate the recording? Perhaps a happy medium is the solution. Until one knows the correct notes, then elaboration upon them is impossible.[9] If the singer has not heard the recording, make sure they first learn what the composer wrote. As they become more familiar with the material, then suggest some vocal elaboration in order to incorporate the correct contemporary style. It is possible they will be able to give some distinctive coloration to the material that is acceptable, but will not be the same as on the recording. Sometimes the singer has learned the music from the recording and tries to create an exact imitation, but they do not have the same vocal skills that are exhibited by the original cast members. Here is where the musical director needs to be able to give guidance to the singer.

In any case, the most important aspect should be that the singer must be able to deliver the song. If this can be done quite convincingly using the notes provided by the composer, this is fine. It is the accepted performance practice of this contemporary musical style to include vocal embellishments, and if this can be done with vocal confidence and stylistic integrity, then the musical director will permit it. This is where one's knowledge of the various theatrical styles is so important, and proves that style can only be acquired through extensive listening and attending of professional musical productions.

Sometimes a character voice needs to be used, such as in "Adelaide's Lament," from *Guys and Dolls*. Some actor/singers can do this easily and they are the people who are right for the part. It is possible to use these character voices without causing any vocal damage. When in doubt, it is best to consult a vocal teacher or vocal coach.

Some women are excellent "belters." This is definitely a Broadway style for many of the roles for women. However, every voice teacher will tell you there is a right way and a wrong way to belt. If the singer belts incorrectly, they will not have a singing voice for very long, and they will surely develop nodules on their vocal chords! Or, they will have a well-developed chest register and perhaps a good top range, but the middle voice which connects the two areas will have vanished. Going between the two registers there will be an abrupt sound shift rather than a smooth transition. For the belter or for the bright sound of Broadway, the more the singer can place the sound high in the mask, high in the face and behind the nose, the better off they will be. You, the musical director, can be of great help regarding vocal production of all members of the cast.[10]

In some ways, belting is associated as being *the* Broadway sound—forward, bright, brassy, slightly nasal, and a sound that projected extremely well over an orchestra in the pre-amplified theatre days. The vocal style was developed early in this century before the days of microphones when it was necessary for the singer to fill the large theatres being constructed at that time. "Since the belt voice is in the chest register and the chest register is an extension of the speaking voice in its conversational range, it was the ideal voice to fill these behemoths of theatres. It finally became a tradition that the Broadway musical should be synonymous with the belt voice coming from chorus girls and leading ladies who were lucky enough to have one" (Silver 1985, 96). One writer commenting on the vocal demands of *West Side Story* noted the operatic range of Bernstein's music "rather than the chest voice of show music" (Stearns 10). Over the years the requirements for the belt voice have stretched higher and higher. The recent Broadway hit, *Side Show,* comes to mind. The range for the female leads has been written so that the women are required to carry the belt voice to notes commonly used in the head register. It is no wonder that the actors need to take time off for vocal rest in order to save their instrument.

It has been my privilege to work with several belters, from student amateurs to New York professionals. Of all these singers, I have met only one soprano who could belt all the way up to a high "g-2" with ease and with good, pleasant vocal quality. This person never had any vocal problems, such as fuzziness in the sound or laryngitis. On the other hand, the more common situation is that you will cast belters who will give their all during rehearsals and knock you dead with their projection. Then, just before going into dress rehearsals, or worse, at the performance time, they will find they are in vocal difficulty and require much needed vocal rest in order to restore their voice. Others will be on the verge of getting "nodes," vocal calluses caused from years of vocal abuse. In any case, this problem could have been avoided by judicious use of the voice during rehearsals. It would have been further avoided through study with a good teacher or vocal coach.

In addition, there are Broadway shows which call for female leads to use what is usually called their "legit" sound. *Oklahoma* and *Carousel* or Maria's songs in *West Side Story* would be examples of shows calling for this vocal style. Whatever style is required by the show, it is the musical director's responsibility to make sure the singers get through all the rehearsals without too much fatigue and use their voices to the best of their ability to portray the character they are playing. To achieve this, the musical director will be assuming the role of a vocal coach: helping with diction, text accent, vowel placement, breathing, consonants, and other vocally oriented techniques.

Just as singers are aware of these various styles, by the same token, instrumentalists need to be aware of a sense of style for the production they are playing. The show may have a dance number which uses a Latin beat, and the percussionist needs to understand that a Mambo is a different musical style from Rock and Roll! If your instrumentalists have never played in a jazz ensemble prior to their pit experience, they may not understand the difference in playing "straight" or "swung" rhythms. If this is the case, it is the musical director's responsibility to educate them.

Style in dance is particularly obvious because it is a visual experience. One would never confuse the choreography of Bob Fosse with that of Agnes de Mille. While both worked on Broadway and both are creators of modern dance, they are totally different in style. A choreographer should try to make the dances for *Chicago* or *Sweet Charity* reflect the style of Bob Fosse who created the original productions. By the same token, the dances for *Carousel* or *Oklahoma* will rely on the work of Agnes de Mille and her ballet oriented, yet thoroughly American, creations. The same parallel can be made in music. While we might recognize that one musical style is different than another, we are not always sure what the elements are that make that difference, and, this is where the difficulty comes for the novice conductor.

Some piano/vocal scores will contain stylistic performance suggestions. A woodwind passage in *Sweet Charity* indicates that it is to be played "like Billy May." Sometimes a performance-style indication will be found in the music: "like Gene Krupa," or "like an MGM Musical." If these styles do not ring a bell, then hearing examples of recordings or watching a video or a film of the musical will be of value to the conductor. And, if the orchestra players are not familiar with some of this music, it will be a good idea for the both conductor and players to do some listening.

I have always enjoyed the audition process and have even attended auditions when I was not the musical director. It is easy to spot those actors who have done a great deal of listening to a variety of Broadway recordings and who understand the concept of style. When an actor auditions for more than one role, they do not read for the two parts in the same way. One might argue that this is just what a good actor does because he understands the differences in the two characters. The same will be true in singing. The person auditioning for Nickie in *Sweet Charity* performs stylistically differently when auditioning for Fiona in *Brigadoon*. Yes, the characters are totally different, but, so is the musical style of the shows. It is this difference that will be extremely evident in the singing of the songs that will illustrate how one understands the concept of style.

If the actor has the opportunity to study voice privately, the teacher should be one who has come to terms with vocal styles. It is important that this teacher be able to "demystify musical theater singing, and learn to teach students to sing freely and healthily, while remaining true to stylistic considerations" (Rosewall 1980, 17). A friend in New York, who does a great deal of vocal coaching, encourages his clients to have songs of various styles in their repertoire. In this way, when a person goes to an audition, he is prepared to sing a variety of types of music depending upon the show for which he is being considered. He may have a contrasting song available should he be asked to perform something of a different style.

There was a memorable instrumental rehearsal early in my musical theatre conducting experience that is pertinent to this discussion. During the rehearsal, there was one section of the music that was sounding acceptable but it was just not right. We stopped, and I said to the orchestra, "The music we are playing is the accompaniment to a ballad of the Big Band era." We started again. My! What a difference in the music when the concept of style had been clarified. Obviously some of the players knew the music of Tommy Dorsey and Glenn Miller and brought this to their playing. Yes, I was working with musicians with some performance experience and not rank amateurs, so the result came quickly. But, even beginning players can achieve this stylistic goal, it may just take a bit longer.

And so, the question is asked once again—how is the concept of style taught to young musicians or incorporated into performance by more experienced players? If the style in question has never been heard, then it needs to be illustrated. It seems this can best be done through recordings. Find a time for the cast and orchestra to hear an illustration if the musical director cannot convey the right idea verbally or illustrate it musically. If necessary, outside help from someone experienced in this area may be required. Some assigned listening would also be appropriate. Even with all this, depending upon the ability of your cast and musicians, the right style may or may not come through.

However, listening to the original cast recordings of musical productions may not be as accurate as you would suppose. Most original cast albums do not include all of the dance music in the show. And, there may be cuts and/or alterations to vocal numbers. These may be due to a time restriction, or it may be that there is stage action that the music covers in the performances which would not make good listening. There have been times when cast recordings have been in different keys than the original score. There are some solos that have recorded as duets. The recording can give one a sense of the style of performance, but the score is still the accurate source guide for performance.

It has been my experience that students majoring in music theatre do a considerable amount of listening and are able to incorporate what they have heard into their own *persona*. Most instrumentalists who are comfortable in the pop/jazz world understand this, too. But, even some of these instrumentalists may not know the excellent instrumental writing of Nelson Riddle and Billy May when performing a musical written in the '40s style. When students have done some listening and understand what they are required to do, the resulting "style" has a chance of being much more accurate.

It is the lack of a sense of style that flaws most amateur productions. However, there is one style that never fails to come across accurately regardless of the performer's abilities or level of experience. This is the country or hillbilly style. Maybe this is why *Li'l Abner* is such a popular show with amateurs or is the first show to perform in places that does not have a tradition of staged performances. Or, it could be that people seem to understand this style because it has been reinforced by what they have seen on television. Understanding the style of Stephen Sondheim, of Noel Coward, or of Boublil and Schönberg requires the same sort of understanding on the part of all participants.

Chapter 10

Blocking

The blocking period of the rehearsal process can be and often is a time of great frustration for the musical director. Here, you will find the chorus and the principals that you have thoroughly trained, who are able to sing enthusiastically and correctly, suddenly sound as if they have forgotten everything! Relax—this is to be expected. Most of all, it is a situation that is to be accepted and tolerated. The music can be quickly refreshed after the blocking period is completed if you have taught it well. During blocking, it is more important that the actors learn where they are to stand or move, and what their motivation and actions are in order to play the scene. They will need time to write down these directions in their scripts as the instructions are being given by the director. The actors' attention should be on these activities, nothing else. But, blocking rehearsals are a very dangerous time musically! It is not uncommon for musical mistakes to creep in as an actor tries to incorporate the blocking given while singing the song. It is a problem for the soloist as well as chorus members. An alert musical director will notice these mistakes and remind the actor of his error.

These musical errors should be corrected sooner rather than later. Do not let musical mistakes go uncorrected even during these blocking sessions. Once music has been incorrectly learned and reinforced with a physical action, the mistaken version will be so strongly supported by the physical movement that the musical error will never disappear! Once a physical gesture has been associated with music (or the music with the gesture), whether the music was learned correctly or incorrectly, it is practically impossible to change. It may be necessary to interrupt the blocking process and have a brief music rehearsal to reestablish and assure musical accuracy. This is one reason why it is a good idea for the musical director to attend *all* blocking sessions as well as all dance rehearsals.

A recent experience working with a choreographer who has Broadway credits comes to mind. The choreographer was teaching a movement that reinforced a particular rhythm pattern in the music. It was presented correctly, but in repeating the movement, the choreographer reversed the rhythm pattern and illustrated it differently than had been taught. The dancers accepted the choreographer's rhythm as correct as they were not using their scores at this time. I was able to state the rhythm correctly for the choreographer, the dancers returned to singing the music using the rhythm as it had been taught, and the inaccuracy was repaired. Had I not been at the rehearsal, the error would not have been discovered until the next full rehearsal. By that time, it would have been too late.

Fortunately, this choreographer did not take my correction of her error personally. I am sure there are directors and choreographers who would not have wanted to be corrected by a musical director! This could be a problem for a director who is new to working in the area of musical theatre, or who has little or no musical sense. Any type of correction will need to be done with great tact.

Full-voice singing during blocking sessions or choreography rehearsals should *not* be encouraged or permitted. It is a waste of vocal energy! If the music has been well-taught and properly learned during the initial musical rehearsal times, it will quickly return to the actors' memories so that they will be able to incorporate the newly taught blocking with the music. However, while blocking is taking place, the musical director should listen carefully to the soft singing to make sure the cast is not making changes in what you have so laboriously taught.

After the blocking has been learned, the musical director should plan to have a music review session to reconstruct the music originally learned regarding phrases and dynamics. This will further assure that the music is well entrenched. It is a good idea to have a music review scheduled during the blocking rehearsal time. This reminds the cast members of the music just before the director or choreographer began adding movement. A short review after blocking is highly recommended, and in most cases, necessary. After reviewing the music, then repeat the number in combination with the blocking that has been assigned. Doing the music and the movement under tempo would be helpful, too. Then bring the number up to speed. After a couple of run-throughs, the number should be secure. Both the blocking and music will require repetition and polishing before it is up to performance level.

As mentioned earlier, cast members will either have scripts which have the full text of the show and the music in the back, or, they will be working from sides, with the music in a separate book. Many actors prefer to rehearse musical numbers by looking only at the words of the song found in the script, rather than at the music section at the back of the book. If they are not music readers, this is acceptable, but if they are musically literate, the cast members should write their blocking notes in the musical portion rather than the text portion of the script. It would even be a good idea for them to make these notations in both places. By always looking at the music, the actor is constantly reminded what the correct pitches are. Even with this precaution, it is still possible that the music will be learned incorrectly.

In giving directions to actors, the director will use terms such as "up stage" or "down stage" or "stage right" or "stage left," or "cross" to indicate the desired movement. It is a good idea if you, the musical director, understand this stage vocabulary and are able to use these terms correctly. It will save a lot of confusion. In rehearsals, it will be necessary to stop in the middle of a musical number for some reason or another. To restart, you may want to go back a bit and could give instructions such as, "Let's begin at measure 45. This is when you sing (give text) and cross down left." Instructions given that clearly will let the cast member(s) know exactly where they should pick up the music.

Many stage terms make a great deal of sense whether or not you have worked in the theatre before. Stage left obviously means the left side of the stage; down stage means toward the audience, etc. Some terms are brand new.[11] However, there was one term used frequently in musicals that confused me for years. This term was "in one." I knew that it referred to action of a scene which took place in front of a drop curtain in the down stage area, but I did not understand why. Here is the answer. The wings (or sides) of a stage are divided into three (sometimes four) entrances (often spoken of as alleys, or openings) for the actors. The entrance closest to the audience is entrance area number one, the next area further upstage is called number two, and the one closest to the back of the stage is number three. In the days before computerized moving of sets and scenery, it was the custom to lower a drop, or pull a curtain across the stage, and play the scene in the space between the drop and the apron of the stage. The actor or actors would make their entrances and exits onto the stage through entrance number one. While the scene was being played in front of the drop curtain, a completely different set was being set up behind the curtain, out of the eyes of the audience, to be revealed when the in-one scene was finished. (Many times, the in-one scene was a song sung by one of the principals, or one or two singers.) Therefore, when a scene is being played in-one, it means in the area at the front of the stage, closest to the audience, with a drop or curtain cutting off the audience's view of the rest of the stage. It is a theatrical term that a musical director needs to add to his vocabulary. These in-one scenes require the same cues to begin and/or stop music: the raising and lowering of the drop or the raising and lowering of lights which coordinate the necessary scene change music into and out of these in-one scenes, just as for the scene that is played on the full stage.

Once the blocking is learned and the scenes are being played, notice whether the singers, especially in duets, are singing too much toward the wings rather than cheating front. As actor/singers, they will want to eye-ball the person with whom they are singing. This is good from the acting point of view, but the sound will go into the wings and be lost. Amateurs will need to be taught how to cheat front in order to project their voices to the audience. This can still be a problem, even when wearing microphones, because members of the company will "find they cannot turn toward the wings or the mike level will drop" (Young 66). This technique of "opening up the scene" gives the audience a better visual perspective of the actor as well.

As has already been mentioned, it is a good practice for the musical director to attend all the blocking sessions rather than taking this time as vacation, assuming that by teaching the music to the cast, his work is finished. There are several reasons for attending all blocking and dance rehearsals. Most directors work from the script when blocking the actors in the scenes. When blocking musical numbers, they will use the script thing rather than referring to the musical score because directors are usually nonmusic readers. In many cases, there are discrepancies between the text of the script and the score. If you are present at these rehearsals, you can point out what is indicated in the score. If the two are completely different, a compromise may need to be reached. In older shows, there can be serious differences. One serious discrepancy comes to mind. The principals had learned the music to a duet as it appeared in the musical books, only to discover at the blocking sessions that the script indicated there was additional text. Since the orchestra parts contained only the sixteen measures in the musical director's score, the director had to alter his original blocking plan. These sorts of differences between script and score are not always so drastic, but it does illustrate the need for teamwork in this business.

By attending blocking rehearsals, the musical director can address other problems as well, such as making sure the music remains as it was taught, not allowing mistakes to creep in. The musical director will want to be on the lookout for blocking that might cause musical problems: are they being asked to sing facing upstage, or into the wings, or are they so far upstage that they will have difficulty hearing the orchestra or being heard over the orchestra? Choreographers love to incorporate turns and spins into their movement. Do these take place when the singers have their most difficult notes to sing? These movements are colorful and attractive, but they can play havoc with the sound! Try and save those movements for the dance routines. Do not sacrifice the sound for any blocking. But above all, work together to achieve the best sound and the best dramatic effect possible!

When all the stage movement has been completely blocked by the director, it is a good idea to call a rehearsal just to confirm that all the music has stayed learned as it was taught. "It is amazing how the musical phrasing, tempos, and dynamics of a score can alter as the actors become more confident with the material" (White 73). This check-up rehearsal is another way of making sure the music remains as it was taught.

If the musical is in production for a number of weeks or months, a recheck rehearsal is a good way of keeping music and dialog at the same level they were taught. At these rechecks, it is not a bad idea to have the cast sing the music of the show using their scores rather than singing totally from memory. Have the cast think their movements as they sing. Strive for the same effects you achieved in the first musical rehearsals—intensity, vitality, accuracy, sharp attacks and releases, clean and clear texts, and, most of all, beautiful singing that reflects the character of the production! If there is time, end the rehearsal(s) with a run through of the singing with the movement. If either the movement or the music fall apart, focus on the areas that need attention and run the number again.

Chapter 11

Some Electronic Help

It has become the accepted practice in most productions, amateur as well as professional, to use either floor microphones placed on the edge of the stage or for the actors to wear body microphones. If microphones are used, the actors should wear them at all dress rehearsals prior to opening, so that they will become comfortable using this equipment just as with using any stage prop. In amateur productions, the body microphones would probably be only worn by principles rather than by members of the chorus. For most professional productions, every member of the cast has a body microphone. When microphones are used, it is absolutely necessary that the musical director and director work very closely with the sound engineer to ensure proper levels of sound. This is especially important when determining the proper balance of the music between singers and the orchestra. In the professional world, the orchestra as well as the singers will be miked. It is no wonder that in these theatres there is a large sound console at the rear of the house which is run by the sound engineer(s) who mixes the sound during the performance.

Today, there is a predilection for overamplification in many professional productions as well as in movie theatres where the sound level is extremely high. One professional actor commented that "Shows are louder and louder, not a development that I am happy with. Unfortunately, the shows are loudest in the balcony. Even straight plays are amplified now, because audiences are used to turning up their TVs and unwilling to take those few moments to adjust their hearing" (Wolfe 1). Audiences do not seem to mind this high level of sound. This writer does not mind hearing the natural, unmicrophoned voice on the stage. But, he defers to the use of amplification due to the size of some theatres, the size of orchestras, and the fact that the use of electronic assistance does prevent straining of the actor's vocal mechanism. Also, present day audiences have become accustomed to hearing amplified/supported sound.

Another piece of electronic equipment needs to be mentioned that may be helpful to the musical director. This is the use of video camera and TV monitors for coordinating off-stage singing. Not ever show requires the chorus to sing off stage, but *Show Boat* and *Joseph and the Amazing Technicolor Dreamcoat* are two that do. Also, there might be a situation in which off-stage cast members could reinforce the singing of the people on stage. In order to assure that the singers backstage and the orchestra in the pit stay together, a video camera will be placed in the pit and focused on the conductor. TV monitors placed in the stage right and stage left wings backstage will allow the singers to gather around the monitor and follow the conductor. It is best to keep the equipment turned on throughout the performance rather than risk not having it ready when the actors need to begin singing. Closed-circuit TV is used in professional theatres in many ways. There are shows in which the orchestra is located behind the performers and the only way to communicate is through the use of TV monitors placed so the performers can see the conductor. In some theatres, these monitors are on the edge of the first balcony. In others, the TV monitors are suspended in the alley entrances so that the chorus can begin singing at the correct time as they come on stage.

The use of sound support for the actors, the use of sound monitors to help the actors on stage hear the orchestra more clearly, and the use of TV cameras and monitors to assist in communication between orchestra and stage are only a few ways electronics can assist a production. We are all grateful that microphones and head-sets allow for communication between the stage manager and the members of the technical crew rather than sending hand-signals from one side of the stage to the other. As the years progress there will undoubtedly be new and more sophisticated uses for these electronic friends.

Chapter 12

Dance Numbers

Most Broadway musicals have one or more big production numbers where there is a lot of dance. Here is an opportunity for the actor/singer to display the third side of their talent, that of dancer. During the rehearsal period, the dance numbers are sometimes rehearsed concurrently with the blocking/scene work, but in a different location. This is an efficient use of rehearsal time, but it is only possible when the same people are not needed in both rehearsals. Dance rehearsals usually take place in a dance studio which has a proper floor and walls of mirrors. The choreographer will be in charge of these rehearsals. If concurrent rehearsals are not possible either due to space or personnel limitations, the director and choreographer will schedule these rehearsals so that adequate times for both are provided. Some high schools rehearse three evenings a week for two hours at a time and have a separate choreography session on Saturday mornings.

The choreographer and the musical director will have already talked about the dance numbers: is there too much music, should cuts be made, if so, where? When can the choreographer have a dance tape? Most amateur productions, whether in high school or community theatre, will not be able to use all the dance music provided in a score. It could be that there is insufficient space on stage for a big production number. It could also be that removing some of the dance numbers is a way of shortening the show. The most frequent reason for not doing all the music in a dance number is that most amateur productions do not have people with the necessary dance training and experience to make these production numbers a success. In these situations, the number will be totally eliminated or altered to fit the capabilities of the particular cast. The items mentioned below will be appropriate whether you plan to use all or only a portion of the dance music.

But, let us assume that for the production under discussion *all* of the music in the dance number will be used. It is the musical director's responsibility to provide a dance tape from which the choreographer can work. Most commercial recordings of Broadway shows do not have all of the dance music on the original cast recording. Therefore, a piano version of the music needs to be recorded so that the choreographer can listen to the tape, get an idea as to how the music goes, and create the dances. The musical director and the rehearsal accompanist are responsible for making these tapes. When making a tape, it is not necessary for the recording to be the definitive performance of the number. Every note on the musical page does not need to be played, but the music should be played in a steady tempo and be rhythmically correct with the basic melody and harmonies. It will be from this tape that the choreographer will work in order to give the dancers the required number of counts. That is why it needs to be rhythmically solid. In an ideal situation, the orchestra would be assembled, rehearse the dance music, and make a recording of the music as the dance tape. This is not possible since the orchestra may not be assembled by the time rehearsals begin and sometimes the orchestral parts do not arrive until a month before the first performance. The choreographer will probably have a considerable amount of work completed before that time. This is another reason for making a dance tape.

When the dance tape is recorded, it will help the choreographer if each selection is announced before the music starts. If there are any verbal cues included in the music give these as well. If there are cuts made in the music, indicate these verbally.

Along with the dance tape, the choreographer should be provided with a copy of the piano/vocal score, or at least copies of the numbers to be staged. Most choreographers do not read music and learn the music from listening to it. If they have heard only the music from the original cast album, they may be surprised to find there is are discrepancies between what they heard and what is in the score. I worked with one choreographer who had a particular idea for the movement and insisted that the music be altered to meet her ideas for the dance. It took some diplomacy to solve that situation.

Once the dance tape is completed, the choreographer can now begin to create the dance material to be used. After studying the score and/or listening to the tape, the choreographer may find that he would like to eliminate a few measures of music, maybe even several pages. If this is the wish, it is the musical director's responsibility to find a smooth way to achieve a good cut in the music. This also means that a new piano tape must be prepared for the choreographer that incorporates the new change. Needless to say, the cut will be marked in the conductor's score and this information will be passed on to all the instrumentalists so that their scores can be marked prior to the first instrumental rehearsal. It is not uncommon to make further alteration in the length of the dance after the first tape has been made.

If a separate accompanist is not available for dance rehearsals, the choreographer will use the dance tape. The ideal situation, of course, would be to have a rehearsal accompanist who will attend all the dance rehearsals and play the music on the piano. Having an accompanist will make dance rehearsals go more smoothly, as it makes starting, stopping, and repeating sections much easier. If changes in tempo are necessary, the pianist can play the music either faster or slower according to the choreographer's wishes.

Once into the dance rehearsals, the choreographer may discover that the dancers are not picking things up quite as quickly as hoped for, and a further cut needs to be made. If this is the case, and it is in agreement with the musical director, another tape needs to be made from which the choreographer can work. Or, if a dance accompanist is used for the dance rehearsals, he will mark the score and play the music as agreed upon. This new information will be passed on to the orchestra members prior to their first rehearsal. This process will continue until the dance music is set.

The ideal musical rehearsal situation would be to have an accompanist for *all* dance rehearsals, and a separate accompanist for all blocking rehearsals and running of the scenes. In that way, the two rehearsals could take place simultaneously, provided the actors were not needed in both rehearsals at the same time.

When possible, I attend all dance rehearsals. First, I enjoy watching the dancers work and am always amazed at how quickly they pick up the dance combinations. And, on occasion, it has been beneficial to be present to settle a musical question that has arisen during the rehearsal. Sometimes, tempo differences have been solved. At other times, cuts in the dance music were made on the spot.

Chapter 13

Rehearsal Pianist

During the musical and blocking rehearsals, it is accepted practice to use a piano as the only musical accompaniment. The person who serves as rehearsal pianist has a tremendous responsibility toward the success of the musical director and the efficient running of rehearsals. Young observes that the rehearsal accompanist is central to the rehearsal progress of a production, because that person must play the right notes and the right rhythm in the right tempo from day one! Young continues, "It is preferable that the rehearsal pianist be a musician who will have the feeling for what [the director] and the musical director are trying to accomplish" (Young 20). Who knows? That excellent pianist who is following your direction may develop into a musical director some day in the future, thanks to your excellent training and example! It has happened before.

The rehearsal pianist must do more than just play the music for the entire show. They must serve as the orchestra during the rehearsals. They must be sensitive to the needs of the performers, and at the same time follow the conducting pattern of the musical director. In many ways, the accompanist is the necessary support for the cast in every aspect of the show. If the accompanist does not follow the musical director, then the singers will learn to depend on the piano rather than the conductor which may cause problems when the orchestra joins the production for the final rehearsals.

There are places in the music where actors may listen to get their cues, such as a flute line, or a particular rhythm pattern. It is helpful to indicate these to the actors. But even in rehearsals, the actors need to feel comfortable following the musical director and learning to watch for his cues. More importantly, the cast must learn "to watch the conductor without being obvious" (Boland and Argentini 164). Learning to catch a cue of the musical director out of the corner of one's eye may be a new skill for some cast members, but when mastered and perfected in blocking rehearsals, it will save time in the dress rehearsals on stage when all the forces are together.

During rehearsals, both the early music rehearsals as well as blocking sessions, the rehearsal pianist may be assisted at the keyboard by another pianist, by reinforcing the melodic line or the harmonic parts. If the accompanist is fully occupied with accompaniment, the melody or vocal parts can be played an octave or two higher by a second person to assist in learning. This can be done even on a second piano if your rehearsal facility has two instruments available. However, a safer rehearsal method would be playing parts and avoiding any accompaniment in order not to confuse the singers with something other than what they should be singing. The playing of parts should be used only in the early stages of learning the music, rather than later in the rehearsal period when the actors should become comfortable with hearing the accompaniment.

An alert accompanist is one of the greatest musical assets a musical director and a production can have. His skills are essential to the smooth running of the show. The accompanist must be alert to the needs of the singers, yet avoid the temptation of following them rather than the conductor. The accompanist must be a music editor as well: playing what is needed and leave out unnecessary notes in the score. It is not necessary for the pianist to try and play every note on the page, and this goes contrary to everything most pianists have been taught. Most pianists are so concerned with playing every note they see on the page, that they lose the rhythmic feel and the tempo will sag. Once the music is securely learned, the rehearsal pianist will be able to add more of the accompaniment. However, for a novice keyboard player, it will take a while to learn that it is more important to keep a very steady beat, with emphasis on the bass line, and fill in with the correct harmonies, even if it means dropping some of the notes on the page. "The best way to help the group is to bang out the left hand," states one professional musical director (Myers 1999). This person was referring to the practice of having the left hand take the place of the bass and percussion, which are normally not available for blocking rehearsals.

All cuts and changes need to be thoroughly marked in the conductor's score as well as the accompanist's score. These must be written in pencil rather than pen, as more changes will undoubtedly be made before the show is set in concrete. Plus, all marks made in rented scripts and scores must be erased before they are returned. A hefty fine is levied by the rental agency for music that has not been erased.

Should a key change be necessary to benefit the singers, it is the responsibility of the musical director to be sure the accompanist has the transposed music. Some pianists are skilled enough to be able to transpose at sight. Others will write only the chords of the new key in the music and will be able to play it correctly. More frequently, it will be necessary to write out the song in the new key on separate paper. Computer technology has made the job of transposition much easier. To make the transposition, it is necessary to enter the music into the computer and indicate what transposition is required. The computer will do the transposition instantly, and print out the music in the new key. The music can be entered using a keyboard connected to the computer through a MIDI-interface or it can be entered manually. Finale is a widely accepted music computer program used by many musicians and publishers. Sibelius is a newer music program which has gained wide acceptance. Both work on IBM as well as MAC platforms.

When the production moves into performance time, the rehearsal pianist must shift from being the only source of accompaniment and assume a totally different role. Now the piano becomes an ensemble instrument and a member of the orchestra. During the long weeks of rehearsal, the pianist was the only musical accompaniment. He *was* the orchestra! Now, the pianist must learn to work with the other instruments playing in the real orchestra. If there is not a separate keyboard book to play from, this shift in roles will require the pianist to adjust totally from what he has been playing in order not to duplicate material played by the instruments. For some pianists, this transition is a time of frustration, for they know the show better than the instrumentalists coming into the "pit." It will take a couple of rehearsals before this adjustment becomes comfortable, but it can be done. The conductor needs to be the final judge as to what the pianist now plays, based upon how the piano balances with the rest of the instruments.

Some shows have separate keyboard books, which could be a piano book, or a celesta book. When a harp is called for, but is not available, this part can be played quite satisfactorily from an electronic keyboard. Many times, the pianist will prefer to play from the piano/vocal score that they have been using during rehearsals rather than from one of the separate keyboard books. In this way, the pianist knows what is taking place in the music at all times. Whether the accompanist plays from the piano/vocal score or from the keyboard part provided is a matter of preference. This is especially true if the full instrumentation is not used. In this case, the keyboard can fill in music that would normally be played by the missing instruments.

Keyboard demands will vary depending upon instrumental requirements of the show. Most contemporary shows require electric keyboards that can produce a variety of sounds. *Grease* uses two keyboards. *Children of Eden* requires three keyboard players: two playing electric and one who plays both electric and acoustic piano. In more contemporary shows, the books for the electric keyboards have indications for harpsichord, harp, percussion, organ, and other wonderful effects. It is highly possible to use electric keyboards to provide sounds for instruments not available. These can vary from some percussion sounds, the harp, even strings.

One further word about rehearsal pianists. In the professional world, it is not uncommon for musical directors to have gained their experience and training by first serving a period of time as a rehearsal pianist. Sometimes, the title assistant musical director will be used. In addition to serving as the pianist for rehearsals, he may conduct performances when the musical director is away. Working as a rehearsal pianist, therefore, is sometimes a stepping stone to the top job.

Chapter 14

Run-Through Rehearsal with Cast

Once the production has been completely blocked, the director will schedule a run-through of the entire show. In all probability, the director has already had a run-through of Act I before moving on to the blocking of Act II. The ideal situation would be for the actors to be off-book and that all the music is thoroughly learned. If this is not the case, the script and music should be very close to that status. Prior to this run-through, the musical director will have appeared in front of the cast at rehearsal in the role of conductor. Any problems regarding tempo have been addressed during the earlier rehearsals, so that bad habits were avoided or corrected before they became too well entrenched. The cast realizes that your job as conductor is to coordinate the music from the orchestra pit with the action on the stage. They should be accustomed to looking for the baton and your conducting gestures, rather than merely listening to the rehearsal pianist for their cues. The cast does not stare at the conductor as a member of a choral ensemble would do. The cast is developing their characters. It goes without saying that by now all tempi should be a performance speed.

The first run-through rehearsal begins with Act I, and following a short break continues with Act II. This first run-through gives an idea of pacing for the entire show, what is going well, and what needs attention. Following the rehearsal, the cast will be given notes from the director, the choreographer and the musical director. Some directors prefer a different plan. Rather than run the entire show at the first run-through rehearsal, the director might run the entire Act I. Then, after a few minutes break, perhaps with some notes to the cast from the director, the choreographer, and the musical director, Act I will be repeated. At the next rehearsal time, the director will do the same procedure only with Act II. Either rehearsal plan produces the same result—a complete run-through of the show.

One can learn many things during the run-through rehearsal. You can get a feeling as to how much time the show will take. The actors begin to see how they fit into the scope of the overall plan, how much time they have for costume changes, where is their next entrance after they exit, and other technical matters. As musical director, you will begin to get a clear picture as to how the various musical numbers fit into the script. You will begin to understand the pacing and tempo of the production. You will also see places where the music needs a touch-up rehearsal.

Chapter 15

Stop/Go Rehearsal with Cast

Once the director has had a complete run-through of the show, he will begin a period of clean-up work. This time of refinement is sometimes referred to as "stop/go." Other people call this type of rehearsal a "work-through" because one "works through" a scene over and over until it begins to take shape. The director will usually start at the top of the show, progressing scene by scene, repeating scenes or sections of scenes over and over in order to achieve the quality needed. There may be a change of blocking during this time. The director will put a great deal of emphasis upon the intentions behind the dialog, the character development, and the playing of action between actors. This is where the real work of the show takes place.

There may be changes for cues for starting musical numbers. During this refinement process, these changes may develop due to alterations in stage direction, or the cast delivering the dialog more quickly because they are more familiar with it.

By this time, the dance numbers will be learned, but will require the same sort of stop/go clean up. The choreographer will do this type of work at a separate dance rehearsal.

During stop/go work, there will be repetitions of music that takes place in these scenes. Many times the scene prior to a musical selection will be repeated until it begins to take the shape desired by the director, stopping just before the actor or ensemble is supposed to go into the musical number. Then the director will repeat the scene, this time including the music. The period of stop/go rehearsals can be a very tedious time for the musical director. He may even feel that it is a waste of time for him to attend and that his presence is not needed at the rehearsal. Just the contrary is true. Stop/go rehearsals are a very important time for the musical director as well, as this is a period of musical refinement just as it is for the acting. Is the song being sung and played in the same mood that the director has been working for with the dialog? It is a time to continue striving to get it right. Based upon what you observe during these rehearsals, it may be necessary to schedule a separate music rehearsal to address matters observed during the stop/go.

Once the stop/go rehearsal period is over, the director will then schedule one or two rehearsals which will be run-throughs of the complete show. The next step for the production is the time when all the elements of the show come together: the full cast, makeup and costumes, the set, the lights, the orchestra, and the technical crew.

It is time for dress rehearsals.

Chapter 16

Accompaniment of the Performance

The decision will have been made very early in the planning process regarding the accompaniment that will be used for the performances of the show. This decision may be made solely on the availability of musicians. A school instrumental program may not include an orchestra, thereby cancelling the availability of any string players. Budget may determine how much money can be spent to hire musicians for the orchestra. Whatever, it should be remembered that "most musicals written before 1960 are intended for full orchestra, which includes a large string section" (Rosewall 1987, 52). The type of show will determine what is the best solution for the accompaniment of the production.

Can a piano be used for performances, just as was used in rehearsals? What about adding a bass and drums to the piano to enhance the rhythmic pulse? Some shows work well with the use of two pianos which give a fuller sound than only one piano, but still retains the single color of the piano. Some musicals have a separate two-piano accompaniment available for rent, but most musicals do not. If the decision has been made to use a two-piano accompaniment but there is not a two-piano score available, the two pianists must improvise an arrangement between them. One solution is to have one pianist play the music in the bass clef, the other pianist play the music in the treble clef, with both pianists filling in when needed. A variety in the piano texture could be achieved with one piano playing alone on one number such as a ballad, while the other piano rests, then reverse the situation. Be sure to have both play for the big dance numbers.

I am going to rule out a viable accompaniment possibility: that of using recorded or "canned" music, a performance practice found in many dinner theatres. There are advantages and disadvantages for using taped music. The biggest advantage is that you have a professional sound for your production, using instruments, effects, and playing in the correct style that you could not duplicate with the instruments available to you. The orchestra is in tune and sounds great. You do not have to deal with inexperienced musicians trying to find the notes. The disadvantage is that you are locked into the tempo of the tape with no flexibility should an actor flub or the chorus wants to sing at a slightly faster tempo due to the excitement of opening night. I would prefer to have a small combo of piano, bass, and drums, or even two pianos, than to use a prerecorded tape. (For further discussion on this, see chapter 11 in Grace Hawthorne's *There's More to Musicals Than Music.*)

A trio consisting of piano, bass, and drum-set is quite adequate for a small theatre as well as for a show that uses a small cast. It may even be preferable to a loud, out-of-tune orchestra that overpowers the singers on stage and distracts from the stage action by its poor sound. A small combo may be the only solution because local instrumentalists are not available, or your budget does not allow for the hiring of all the musicians called for in the score. Please do not assume that if a trio is used with the pianist playing from the piano/vocal book, the bass player looking over the pianist's shoulder, and the drummer just filling in, that this would be a legal accompaniment. The combo will need to have the instrumental parts provided by the rental agency and should play from this music. You could even add a trumpet or a clarinet to the combo giving some color and variety to the sound. This arrangement will still require the same license for performance. This is clearly stated in the front of the piano/vocal score. For example, on the page listing the instrumentation of *A Chorus Line,* there is the following statement, "The purchase of this score does not constitute permission to perform. Applications for performance of this work, whether legitimate, stock, amateur or foreign, should be addressed to the licensing agent" (Hamlisch 3). In this case, anyone wishing to perform this musical would contact Tams-Witmark. Similar statements are found in other published scores giving the name of the person and/or the address of the agency to contact for permission.

How do you obtain the instrumental parts? Remember that earlier in this discussion, it was stated that a contract arrangement must be made with the licensing agency granting rights to a performance. Six weeks to two months prior to performance, the scripts and chorus books for the show are received, along with one or more copies of the piano/vocal score. A month before the performance date, the copies of the individual instrumental parts arrive. The Rodgers and Hammerstein Rental Library catalog states "materials for amateur productions are delivered two months prior to your opening date: material for professional productions are delivered one month prior to opening (Rodgers and Hammerstein 3, 4). A full set of parts is usually sent with each contract, even if you mentioned at the time the contract was signed that you would not be using a full orchestra. Rental agencies send the full set of parts as a matter of course, rather than breaking up the sets to meet specific instrumental needs and requests. The only time a set may be broken is when there is a request for an extra part in addition to those in the packaged set. If one wishes to have the music sooner, in order to have a longer rehearsal time with the instrumentalists, this can be arranged with the licensing agency, but it could require an additional rental fee.

When the music arrives, check the contents of the box against the invoice, just to make sure you received what you requested. If is a good idea to look closely at the piano/vocal score also labeled as the conductor's score. Even though the previous user is supposed to have erased the marks he made before returning the music to the agency, you can sometimes find traces of these markings. I have discovered that these markings have given me some good ideas about cuts that were made by other productions. In other cases, I have asked myself why that cut was made, as it did not seem to make any sense!

This box of instrumental parts usually contains one instrumental book for each of the instruments required, with one or more copies of each of the string books. When two instruments play off the same score, such as Trumpets I & II, it is a good idea to request a second copy of the same book from the agency. The best time to request extra copies of any part is when making the contract arrangements, rather than after the music has already arrived. It saves on postage and time to receive everything at once. Since the book for Trumpets I & II is usually written together, having two copies of the music allows each player to practice separately. In performance, however, the two players usually prefer to play off the same book. Remember, as musical director, it is not your responsibility to request the music. When all the contractual agreements have been signed, the parts will arrive automatically about one month before the show's opening unless a special request has been made.

The instrumental parts can be handwritten or printed. These handwritten parts are not always easy to read and often contain errors. It will take a bit of practice for the novice instrumentalists to adjust to this style of written music. The more popular shows, such as *Fiddler on the Roof*, *Oklahoma*, and *My Fair Lady*, have printed parts. Thanks to modern technology, some agencies are providing computer generated instrumental music that has the quality of engraved music. Even these are not totally free from error. But, they are a welcome change from the handwritten music commonly used in older musicals.

As musical director, it is a good idea to look through the parts prior to the first instrumental rehearsal. You can anticipate questions that might arise as well as find problems in reading the music.

Chapter 17

The Piano/Vocal Score

So far, the term, piano/vocal score has been used frequently. If available, the piano/vocal score can be purchased in a music store as well as ordered from the music publisher. The piano/vocal score is the volume of music, sometimes called a piano/conductor score, that contains all the music of the show—music for chorus, for solos, play-offs, overture, curtain-call music, and exit music. The music is in the order in which it appears in the show. The piano/vocal score is compact and easy to carry as well as easy to read. It condenses the full instrumental score into a single piano reduction, which makes life easy for the rehearsal accompanist. But, this condensation makes it hard for the Conductor to know exactly which part of the music each instrument should play. The practical effect on rehearsals is that the conductor spends the first instrumental rehearsal with the orchestra simply trying to find out who actually plays which notes (Grote 32). This sounds like a daunting task, but becomes quite easy with experience.

One of the reasons the first instrumental rehearsals are frustrating for any conductor, but especially for the novice, is that you do not always know who plays what because you are not seeing a full orchestral score, or partiture, in the proper sense of the term. The music is not written in open score with a separate line for each instrumental part. Once, after a performance, a member of the audience asked if she might take a look at the score I was using. Before I could place it into her hands, she lamented that for the production she had just conducted she had only received a piano copy to use. This was her first conducting experience and was somewhat relieved when she looked at the piano/vocal score I was using. If your instrumentalists have played in pits previously, they will understand your situation and will be tolerant when you ask a question such as, "Who plays the melody at measure 40?" After the musical director has conducted a couple of musicals, he will be able to see a three-voice-chord written in bass clef which has the cue for "brass" written above the music and assume it will be for three trombones. Or, if the chord is written in treble clef along with the same brass indication, that it will be for three trumpets.

The piano/vocal score contains none of the script. It will have only one or two phrases of dialog which the actors say as a cue before the music should begin. (You will come across scores of shows that contain all the dialog inserted between the musical numbers. Many of the Gilbert & Sullivan operettas are published in this format.) There could be some musical indications in the music of the piano/vocal score, such as "flute" or "strings," written in various places which will allow the conductor to at least know which family of instruments is scheduled to play. These indications are helpful, but are not always accurate.

Some shows do not have a published piano/vocal score that can be purchased. They only provide music that can be rented. In this case, the conductor's score is a manuscript version written on three or four staves rather than the usual two. It contains more of the instrumental cues. The words "reeds," "strings," or "brass" will be written in the score, but in no way does it tell the conductor what specific instrument to cue, only the family. Occasionally, you will find cues to specific instruments, such as, "Trumpet I" or "Trombone II," but these instances are rare. It is not uncommon to find cues for instruments for which there are no parts. These notes are remnants for an instrument that was used while the show was still in rehearsal before it was set. These manuscripts books are not always easy to read as the calligraphy varies in clarity. These scores are large and bulky to carry. Sometimes the music for Act I will be in one volume, with the music for Act II in another volume.

One good thing about scores for musicals is that they usually have either measure numbers or rehearsal numbers in both the piano/vocal score as well as the instrumental parts. These numbers are not always consecutive. Instrumental parts could have both—numbers as well as rehearsal letters. If you are conducting from a printed score which only has rehearsal letters, it will be helpful to take the time and number the measures in your score. This will save valuable rehearsal time when speaking to the orchestra regarding notation in specific measures.

There is another helpful item for you to write into your copy of the piano/vocal score. That is an indication for the act and scene that each musical number takes place. Next to the title of the number write I/4 to indicate that this song takes place in Act I, scene four. Or write II/3 for music in Act II, scene three. When the director announces he would like to run all of Act I, scene four you might draw a blank regarding which musical numbers are involved. A quick glance at the marks you made in your score will refresh your memory.

As mentioned above, in both the piano/vocal score and the instrumental parts there may be skips in the numbering sequence. This disruption of the numbering sequence occurs because there will be places where measures have been cut out. Rather than recopy the entire song, the original numbering was kept, but now there are some numbers gone. It is not uncommon to see measures numbered: 23, 24, 25, then instead of 26, the next numbers will be 43, 44, 45. When the music is played, it makes musical sense.

There will be places where measures have been inserted. For instance, the composer wanted to add four measures before the opening measure. Rather than recopy the entire number, the four measures were given letter names, A, B, C, D and were inserted before the measure one. In this case, the song would begin with measure A, followed by measures B, C, D with the next measure being measure 1.

It is equally common to find measures inserted into the music at various places. In this case you could find the measure numbers going something like: 5, 6, 6A, 6B. These inserted measures are the remains from when the creation of the show was still in progress and the score had not yet been set. (See Example 17-1.)

In rehearsals, a frequently asked question from an instrumentalist will be, "How many measures are between 100 and 109?" This is especially true if the player has rests. The answer to the question could be ten measures or it could be two measures. It depends. The variation could be that a measure was omitted in the copying process, or due to some other error. It could be that a few measures were cut out and rather than change the numbers for the remainder of the music, all measure numbers stayed the same with the exception of the measures cut out. I remember one horrible experience when the conductor's score and the parts did not agree. On this occasion, the conductor's score contained fifteen measures between rehearsal letters A and B, while the instrumentalist parts showed thirty measures. But, the problem was, which of their thirty measures were the same as those in the conductor's score? It took at least twenty minutes of valuable rehearsal time to solve this dilemma by painfully comparing each measure one at a time until the solution had been reached! Despite the conductor's frustration,

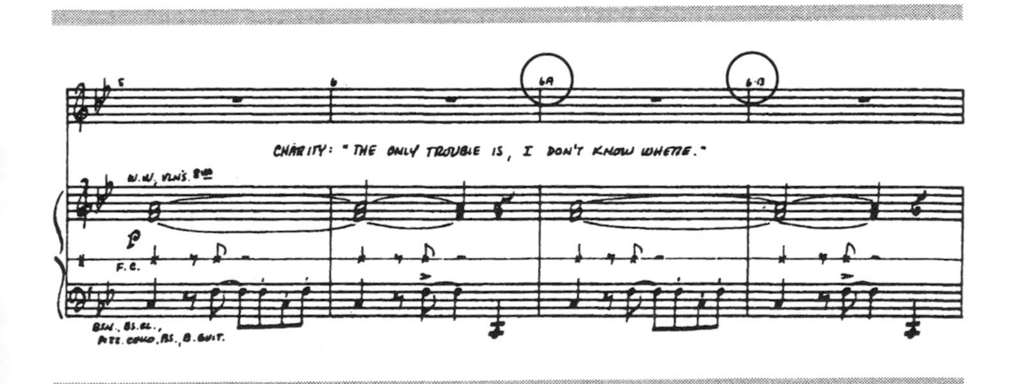

Example 17-1. Last Line Showing Inserted Measure Numbers from *Sweet Charity (used with permission)*

a good lesson was learned. It illustrated the necessity of looking through the instrumental parts prior to rehearsal.

In handwritten rental material, one will often see the letters V.S. at the end of the page of both the instrumental parts as well as the conductor's score. This abbreviation is for *Volti subito* or "turn quickly." This is something that keyboard players and singers rarely encounter as their music is normally printed to the end of the page and you manage the page turns the best way you can. For instrumentalists, the music is often laid out in such a way that page turns can be negotiated during the measures of rests when they are not playing. By careful planning, the copyist can arrange the music on the page so that "the player has at least a measure or two of rest for turning the page" (Read 442). The abbreviation, V.S., is a cue to the player, that although there are a couple of beats of rests at the end of the line, he needs to turn the page quickly and be prepared to play again at the top of the next page.

As mentioned earlier, you will receive the full set of instrumental parts one to two months prior to the performance dates, unless otherwise specified at the time of contractual signing. A full set of parts usually consists of the items listed in Example 17-2.

Piano/Vocal score.

Reed Books—There will be 3 to 5 of these for various woodwind instruments.

Brass Books—These will be in various combinations (3 trumpets, 3 trombones; 2 trumpets, 2 horns, 1 trombone and tuba).

Drums—Usually only one player is needed on drum-set, plus all the effects, such as crotales and cowbell. If Timpani and mallet percussion is called for, this music is in a separate book and will need to be performed by a separate player.

Piano or Keyboard—This could be separate book, or a duplicate of the piano/vocal book.

Guitar

Harp

Strings—Violins; violas; cello; bass.

Example 17-2. Full Set of Parts

How do you know what the orchestral demands are for the show you are to conduct? The instrumentation of the show is often listed on the front page of the piano/vocal score you purchase. You can also consult the licensing agency's catalog, which gives a synopsis of the show, the number of principal roles for men and women needed in the cast, as well as the instrumental requirements of the orchestra (see the sample page for *Guys and Dolls* illustrated in Example 3-1 on page 14). A phone call to the licensing agent will put you in contact with the rental department, which can also give you the correct instrumentation. However, even then, it is possible to receive incorrect information. For example, when inquiring about the requirements for a particular show, one agent indicated the reduced instrumentation for a small combo was the only one available. When speaking with a different agent on a later phone call, it was discovered that there was a full orchestra version available, which was much better than the reduced version.

As has just been mentioned, some shows will have two sets of instrumental parts available: the full Broadway instrumentation, and the alternate or reduced instrumentation. There could be a two-piano version available which may be better for your particular situation. The agent should be able to clarify the differences between the two orchestral versions. Often, the arrangements are not interchangeable; e.g., you cannot use the clarinet part from the full orchestration as the clarinet part for the reduced instrumentation version. You must use one set or the other. Not all small instrumentation arrangements are satisfactory; others are excellently prepared. If possible, you might wish to consult with other people who have performed the show and learn from their experience which instrumental edition was used and why.

At any rate, when you have the instrumental parts, it is up to you as musical director to determine if you will use the full orchestra, or if you will use only piano, bass and drums, as discussed earlier; or a flute, clarinet, trumpet, and trombone along with piano, bass, and drums to provide the necessary accompaniment to the production. You have the music, you know the abilities of the cast, and you know the availability and talents of the instrumentalists that you can use. You make the decision regarding the size of the orchestra and budget.

Chapter 18

String Books

Strings add wonderful color to the orchestration of a show, yet can cause the most problems for a musical director if you do not have trained players because of tuning problems. In order to have the best string sound, it is absolutely necessary to have at least four to six violins. Not all shows call for violas, but one or two are the minimum. You will need one or two cellos, and a bass. Most high schools and communities do not have adequate string players available locally, nor do they have funds to hire them. If the string players are solid musicians, one can achieve excellent effects with two violins and a cello, along with the other woodwinds and brass. It is likely that the winds, brass, and percussion are more readily available within the enrollment of a school or available in the community. Here again, you need to discover what you need, what is available, and build from there.

The violin books are sometimes split into two books and labeled violin AC and violin BD (Violin I and Violin II). In actuality, this means there are four different violin parts because each book is written for *divisi* playing. Some shows put all the violin music in one book and you are provided with two or more copies of identical books. The music will be written on two staffs so that the first violins play the top line, the seconds play the bottom line. Each line may be split into two parts, thus providing four violin parts. There are normally two players to a stand reading off the same book, in the same manner as in classical symphonic orchestras. If one has more than four violins in the pit, which would be wonderful, it will require ordering additional violin books.

The other string instruments have their own separate books: a book for viola, a book for cello, and one for bass. The rental agency will provide one book each for each of these in a set of parts unless additional copies are requested. There is not always a separate book for the viola, as this area has been covered by the orchestrator using lower violin parts.

If you do not have the required number of violins available for your pit, you may find that the inclusion of a single cello or a violin will add a considerable richness to the sound of the ensemble when used in combination with the brass and woodwinds. These two strings (used singly or in combination) add a legato character which is needed for ballads. Try, when possible, to include *all* strings parts in your orchestra.

There have been a few shows I have conducted when a cello was the only string available other than the double bass. This single string gave a sonority to the orchestra that greatly enhanced the overall sound. Of course, it would have been better had I been able to use the entire string contingent, but using a single cello was a definite plus.

You may have to decide whether to use an electric or acoustic bass, depending upon which is available to you. Most conductors prefer the sound of an acoustic bass for older shows and the electric bass for more contemporary productions. But, if an electric bass is all that is available, it can work very effectively even in vintage musicals if it is played well and not too loudly. There are some shows (*Grease*; *Bye, Bye, Birdie,* and parts of *Sweet Charity*) that require the sound of an electric bass.

Chapter 19

Reed Books

The requirements made upon the reed players in musicals can be confusing for the novice conductor. This is because reed players are frequently expected to double on more than one woodwind instrument. Some books indicate instrumental substitutions written in the various reed books as alternatives should the player not be proficient on the instruments indicated.

There are commonly five reed books. Reed I is usually a flute/piccolo book, but could include passages for clarinet and alto saxophone. Reed V is a bassoon, or bass clarinet/baritone saxophone book. Reed books II, III, and IV are for various other woodwind combinations: alto sax, clarinet, oboe; tenor sax, flute, clarinet, etc. If the show is of the *Carousel* or *Oklahoma* vintage, the orchestration will rely heavily on the strings and the woodwind players are not required to double. Each woodwind plays from the assigned book for his instrument, such as a book for only flute/piccolo I, and one for flute/piccolo II if more than one flute is used. There will be a separate book for clarinets. If more than one clarinet is used in the orchestration, each instrument will have its own book. There will probably be a bassoon book along with the usual brass and percussion parts.

If the show is written in a jazz style, such as *Hello, Dolly*, or *Pajama Game*, or *City of Angels,* it is assumed that the reed players will be able to double. In these cases, the instrumentation for the reed books might look like Example 19-1.

Reed I	–	flute/piccolo, alto saxophone, clarinet
Reed II	–	clarinet, flute, alto saxophone
Reed III	–	oboe/English horn, flute, tenor saxophone
Reed IV	–	clarinet, tenor saxophone
Reed V	–	bassoon, baritone saxophone, bass clarinet

Example 19-1. Possible Instruments Required by Woodwind Players

Ideally, you will be able to find players who can play all the instruments needed for each reed book. A theatrical notice in a recent issue of the *Washington Post* advertised for instrumentalists for a forthcoming musical production. The ad indicated that the theatre preferred to hire musicians with musical theatre experience and had openings for percussionists, keyboardists, and reed triplers (Toby's G-7). In other words, the theatre expected the woodwind players to be competent on at least three different woodwind instruments!

To assist players who may not play all the required instruments called for in a book, some reed books will have passages written on a double-lined score. This allows either of the two instruments to play the same part as each is written for the instrument indicated. For example, the double-lined part may be written for bassoon on one line and for bass clarinet on the other. If you have no bassoon, the bass clarinet reads from that line, thus covering the part. Another frequently double-lined book is for the oboe or clarinet. Example 19-2 below shows a double-lined passage which a clarinet could play if no alto-flute were available.

Example 19-2.
Double-Lined Passage of Reed I Book from *Sweet Charity*
(used by permission)

In every case, each double-lined part is written in the correct transposition. The musical director *must* look through each separate instrumental part to determine what the instrumental requirements are. By checking the various reed books, the musical director will see where double-lined passages are written. This may eliminate the need of one of the instruments indicated.

If doublers are not available and if the passage in question is not double-lined, it may be necessary to write out the transposition of the part for the instrument covering that particular book. This will change the color and instrumental texture of the show and would be used only as the last resort. A more common practice for multi-instrument reed books is to use two players on one book in order to have all the instruments needed to cover the part. A flute player and a clarinet player could play from the same book, each playing only the sections written for his instrument, or a clarinet player and a saxophone player could do the same thing. This works well and is a good solution when there are no doublers available, provided both instruments are used equally. Otherwise, players can easily become very bored waiting for the next time their instrument is used.

It is completely possible to perform a show without all the various reeds required, using only the more readily available flutes and clarinets. It is not uncommon for orchestras to use two or three woodwind players and take selections from the five different reed books, thus creating your own parts. The players would juggle the different books among them.

Chapter 20

Brass, Percussion, and Keyboard Books

The books for brass are very straightforward compared to the reed books. There are usually parts for two or three trumpets, normally written in B-flat. There is one book for Trumpet I/II and a separate book for Trumpet III. Because the parts for Trumpet I/II are written in the same book, you might wish to request two copies of that particular book at the time the contract is signed. This would allow each player to have his own copy in order to practice separately. Some shows call for four trumpets. When this is the case, Trumpet IV is a separate book.

The usual number of French horns in most orchestras is two. However, some shows use no horns, some only one, and some as many as three. In older orchestrations, the two horn parts were written in one book with Horn I playing the top line and Horn II playing the bottom. When this was the case, I always requested two copies of the horn book as I found horn players preferred to play off their own book rather than share.

Now that the rental agencies are replacing many of the handwritten parts of older shows with computer generated copies, one is more likely to find that there are separate books for each instrument. The trumpets and horns in this case no longer have to share books—thus making it easier for everyone.

Trombone books are written separately: one book for Trombone I, one book for Trombone II, and one for Trombone III, if that part is called for. Some shows call for tuba which would come as a separate book as well. It is not uncommon for the tuba part to be combined with the Trombone III book. In that case, the player covering Trombone III is expected to be able to double on both instruments.

Some shows make a distinction between the drum book and percussion book. A drum book usually refers to the part played by a drum-set player, while the book for percussion is for the player of timpani and mallet percussion instruments. If there is only one player, the book may be labeled drums or it may be labeled percussion, but the part will be for drum-set with the drummer having indications for cowbell, triangle, and other percussion effects. Sometimes there will be a single drum/percussion book, but it requires two players. The Percussion 1 part is on the top line, Percussion II on the bottom. In this case, you will want to be sure that the agency sends two books for these players to use. In some cases, the drum-set player will be required to shift and play a mallet instrument. This would be in passages where the drum-set is not used.

It is not unusual for players of other instruments to be asked to play a percussion instrument on one or more numbers when their own instrument is not being used. This could vary from a playing a few measures on the claves before returning to their own French horn part. Or, if their instrument is not in a particular number, they might be asked to play the entire number on a bongo.

There will be a separate book for guitar. The orchestra for *Man of LaMancha* requires two acoustic guitars which give the show that special sound. *Children of Eden* calls for two guitars: electric and acoustic. In some shows, the guitar parts can be eliminated without affecting the orchestral texture. In other shows, they are an essential part of the orchestral sound.

A harp book will be called for in some shows and this instrument adds a wonderful color to the sound of the orchestra. If a harp is not available, a worthy substitute is the synthesizer set up to sound as a harp.

The keyboard book could be for piano, for organ, or for celeste. Some shows do not require a keyboard part. Some conductors use a piano in the pit to reinforce the orchestra. Newer shows require one or more keyboards, usually electric, with indications for various special effects. In these instances there will be notations in the part such as "church," "pad," or "Rhodes" to indicate the type of sound to use. These are usually programmed into the keyboard and the player calls them up by punching in the right number or button. The synthesizer has been used in some situations to replace the sound of strings as well as other instruments.

All of the instrumental books will contain cues from other instruments. Depending upon whether you are using the full instrumentation, you might wish to have these cued parts played to fill in for missing instruments. At the first rehearsal, an instrumentalists may ask, "I have English horn cues. Should I play them?" It will be the musical director's decision to have the cues played or ignored. During the rehearsal, you may notice which instruments are not playing during a particular section. If they have no cue written into their part, only rests, this could be a good place to have them fill in a part from another book. Or they could write in a part for these blank measures. This is particularly helpful if you have no strings and are using only brass, woodwinds, percussion, bass, and piano.

What do you do when the big ballad comes along, which is written for string accompaniment, except for a brass chord tag at the very end, and maybe a couple of flute or clarinet solos? This is a good time to fill in from the string books for the clarinets and flutes to play. Keep in mind that clarinets are "transposing instruments" and cannot play directly from a violin book in the same key as the piano. The musical director then becomes responsible for either writing out the transposed part for the players to use to fill in, or for seeing that the players write it out correctly unless they are capable of transposing at sight. Usually the players find this a challenge and take to it quite readily. They find it a game to play from a couple of violin books plus their own reed book. The total omission of strings and use of only brass and reeds can yield a very rewarding and satisfactory pit. By no means does this substitution of instruments give the correct sound to the accompaniment, and should be used only when absolutely necessary. When you have a choice, you will always want to use the original instrumentation.

The area of sound effects usually falls within the realm of the technical staff, but sound can just as well be generated within the pit by programming the synthesizer. These cues may not be a part of the musical score, but are found in the script. The cues will not be called by the stage manager, but are cued by the conductor. The use of thunder in *Children of Eden* is indicated in the piano/vocal score. In *State Fair* a car horn and a bell sound were in the script, but were moved to the pit to be played on a synthesizer. The cues for these sounds were visually determined by the action on the stage. The conductor watched for the stage action, and cued the person at the keyboard who played required sound. The *State Fair* examples took place when there was no music being played, only spoken dialog.

Chapter 21

Locating Instrumentalists
or The Pit Personnel

You have looked through all the instrumental books for the show. You have decided what instruments you are going to use for the accompaniment. Now, you need to locate your players. This area may fall under the jurisdiction of the instrumental director of the school. If you are going to be the show's conductor (and it is strongly recommended that the musical director be the conductor since he will have worked with the show from audition through dress rehearsals) you may want to seek the assistance of the instrumental teacher in locating players. This person may even be willing to prepare the instrumentalists for you . . . but do not count on it. This type of offer can be filled with false promise. Your idea of preparation may be miles apart from that of your colleague!

Locating instrumentalists is not often a problem at the university or conservatory level. Ensemble credit is sometimes awarded for participation in a production. Many students enjoy this type of playing and seek out opportunities to be involved.

For community productions, signs could be placed in the community for instrumentalists, or you could place an advertisement in local newspaper as well as make an announcement on local radio or TV. Your announcement should include a telephone number where more detailed information can be obtained, which should include: the dates for the instrumental rehearsals, the dates and times of all dress rehearsals, and the dates and times of the performances.

Pit playing is an excellent learning experience for young instrumentalists, and you will want to give opportunity to as many people as possible for this. The players you want for your performances need to be quick, alert, able musicians. You do not want to be inflicted with incompetent players. Your singers and actors have worked too hard and long to be hampered by an orchestra that plays poorly. Request and demand the best!

Finding the best drummer available will be of prime importance in selecting members of the pit. A drummer is more important to the success or failure of a pit orchestra staying together than is first evident to an inexperienced conductor. I have a theory regarding the role of the drummer. While conducting the show, I feel that I am really conducting the drummer, who in turn drives the orchestra. That unflagging steady beat, whether the music be fast or slow, is a crucial factor in the success of any musical. The bass player is equally essential in giving the harmonic foundation and rhythmic drive to the music. I would not want to give the impression that these are the only important instruments in a pit, but these are two positions where it is absolutely necessary to have competent players.

And a good drummer does more than is just written on the page. After a couple of rehearsals, he will begin to have a feel for the music and can insert just the right "licks" into his playing that will kick-off a phrase at just the right time. For the success of one production, it was my unhappy task to dismiss a drummer after two rehearsals. He just could not cut it. I was all prepared to go into tech rehearsals without a drummer as this was better than having a weak player. Just before the next rehearsal, an excellent drummer became available whose playing solidified the orchestra making all the difference. We got more accomplished during the third rehearsal than in the other two combined—just because the drummer was the right glue that held everything together.

Having key players or "ringers" in each of the sections will make weaker, less experienced players sound better than they really are. Every instrument is important in a pit, and it is essential to have a good drummer and bassist. A good first trumpeter is the icing on the cake. If your first trumpet is a crackerjack player and the other two trumpets are not as strong, your trumpet section will still sound strong. Therefore, with the following strong players: drummer, bass, and trumpet, you will be headed to a successful pit.

Chapter 22

Cuts in the Score

Before you make any cuts in the score, or even begin your first instrumental rehearsal, you will need to take time to do some marking in your own score. Some piano/vocal scores that you purchase do not contain rehearsal letters or measure numbers. If they have any, it is more likely they will have rehearsal letters, but not measure numbers. (The rented piano/vocal scores usually have these indications.) It will be worth the time to take a string book, or any instrumental part for that matter, count the measures and write in the rehearsal letters and/or measure numbers. Valuable time will be saved in the instrumental rehearsals if these are in your score, as this allows for efficient use of time. When you stop you can give directions accurately as to the location of a particular problem, or more importantly, when you stop, you can get started again without having to go back to the beginning. You can also give specific directions: "four measures after letter A," or "begin at measure 84," or the like. I well remember conducting a show in which the rehearsal letters in the instrumental parts of the woodwinds did not agree with the rehearsal numbers in the brass parts. My! What frustration that was until we discovered why we could never begin in the middle of the number and always had to go back to the beginning. In another show, the music in the piano/vocal score did not agree with what was in the parts for the orchestra! For example, the conductor's score showed that the piece was forty-eight measures, the orchestra had eighty-six measures. Or, the amount of music between rehearsal numbers between the two did not agree. It took a great deal of patience to count measures and get the orchestra parts to agree with the conductor's score. A lot of valuable rehearsal time was wasted!

Cuts are often made in a score either because dance numbers are too long and cumbersome, or the director wishes to omit a section of the show for a particular reason. Part of the problem in making a cut using only a piano/vocal score is that what looks like a logical cut may be in the middle of a very nice trumpet solo, or the flute line, which does not make sense for the instrumentalist. Or, the instrumentation may be different for the first eight measures than for the second eight measures even though the music in these two sections is identical. Try to make cuts at ends of phrases, or at key changes. A musical is usually built on melodies of 8-measure phrases.[12] Phrase length, of course, will vary, especially in more modern shows. As you examine the score, looking for places to make cuts, be aware of cadential patterns and modulations. A dance number may begin in one key with a theme, modulate, then return to the original key. Eliminating the passage in the other key might make an excellent cut, but, again, that could be the place that is much more interesting musically with more colorful orchestration!

Another help in choosing where to make cuts is to look through the parts you have rented and see if there are hints to what has been done in another production. The shadows of erased pencil markings left by others may give a clue where previous musical directors have made good cuts. But, you can also look at these and wonder why they were done that way! Some cuts are easily made while others can cause great anguish.

How much should one cut? This is where the team-approach is essential. It is best to know if the choreographer wishes to do the entire dance number or only part of it, or if the director wishes to make musical changes. This will determine what you will suggest as being cut. Frequently, you will make the most logical cut in the world, only to learn that the choreographer wants more (or less) music. It is quite possible to completely cut out a repeat sung by the chorus that the director is planning to use. A compromise can be reached.

Finally, to determine where cuts can be logically made, play through the music in question or have someone play for you, if you are not competent at the keyboard. It is always best to have the orchestra play it if you have doubts about the piano score. Listen for melodic fragments which could be used. Sometimes things show up in the instrumental parts which are not visible with only the piano/vocal score. Try to determine how much music needs to be used or eliminated. Try to make cuts at places where the 8-measure building blocks of phrases fit well together.

Sometimes a cut works, but the key relationship does not. You can create a good modulation by looking for common chords and similar phrase structure. You can create logical modulations with a couple of accidentals to get you into the key you need. You may need to write out these transitions for your orchestra. If so, copy them on to manuscript paper and make copies to distribute among your instrumentalists, who will write this into their individual parts. Work with your rehearsal accompanist to locate these places if you do not feel comfortable at the keyboard. Play through them a couple of times. If you like it, if it meets the director's approval and that of the choreographer, then inform the instrumentalists, and it is set in concrete.

A sure-fire way to make a cut from one section to another section, especially if the key relationship is not good, is the "quick and dirty" method. To make a cut using this method, merely insert one or two measures of a snare drum roll or drum solo played in the same tempo as the rest of the piece. The other instrumentalists will rest for these drum measures, then continue playing at the next indicated place. This type of cut usually works best in dance numbers.

Once cuts have been determined, this information should be written up for the instrumentalists to write into their scores. The customary practice for making these changes in the various parts is for each player to mark his own part. This *must* be done in pencil, as it is a requirement for each person to erase any marks made in the parts before the music is returned to the rental agency. Some creative students have discovered that Post-Its work just as well for indicating any written change in the part. When it comes time to erase the music, all that is required is to easily remove the Post-Its from the page. By using the various color Post-Its, the instrumentalist can quickly follow a cut from one color to the next color. Some use one color for making musical dynamic notes, such as *piano* or *marcato,* or any indication of that type, and a different color to indicate a cut, thus avoiding confusion. The small size Post-Its are best for this sort of thing, but the larger sized Post-Its can be torn in half to indicate cues. Those who have used it find it works quite well.

If you are working with a choreographer who reads music, he may have sufficient musical knowledge to suggest a cut. In this case they will ask, "May we cut from here to here?" If it meets your approval, then it is a done deal. In my experience, this is a rare situation. By contrast, working with a well-versed, musically-trained person is a true joy. Just by looking at what the choreographer has suggested may open another possibility for the cut that you will not have seen because you are looking at the score, and the choreographer is counting measures or beats.

You may have discovered, during the rehearsal period, that it is better to transpose a song or section of a song, to a key that will better suit a performer's voice. Whenever changes need to be made, inform the musicians as quickly as possible so that they will have time to work out the necessary transposition or rewrite their part. Many pit players can make transpositions of a half-step or a step up or down at sight. Less experienced players will need to write it out. If a transposition is a third or a fourth, either direction, most players will write this out on separate paper and insert in their score. Or, you can write them out for the instrumentalists, using Finale or Sibelius, should time permit.

When signing the contract with the licensing agency, you have agreed to perform the musical that you have rented in its entirety. This is certainly not always possible. Therefore, it seems to be the accepted practice to make alterations in the score to fit your particular needs and situation. These are usually done in the dance numbers because amateur productions (and some professional) cannot negotiate the long dance sequences that are a part of the original Broadway production. Technically, any cut that is made in the score needs to have permission of the licensing agency. The other alteration that one might make in a score will probably be in the transposition of one or more of the solo numbers. This transposition of material for a particular character is made because the voice range of the professional singer in New York City is different from the person cast in the same role for your high school or community production. Music Theatre International provides this transposition service for a fee. At this writing, there are sixteen titles in their catalog where this service can be obtained which includes the song for the piano/vocal score as well as the instrumental parts.

Productions that have taken the time to write the agency indicating that a change was needed in the score, have usually been given permission. Asking is the correct procedure for these situations.

Chapter 23

The First Instrumental Rehearsal

It is the responsibility of the musical director or the pit manager to distribute the music to the instrumentalists which will allow sufficient time to look over the music before the first orchestra rehearsal. Included with the music should be a list of cuts and changes, repeats if not already marked in the music along with any transpositions that might be required. Marking the parts is excellent work for your assistant to do. If you cannot make the notations in the music, a list of the changes on a separate sheet will allow the player to mark his own score. Giving the changes in advance will make the first rehearsal go more efficiently. It goes without saying that when the music is first distributed, a list of dates and location of rehearsals and performances is to be included.

For the first orchestra rehearsal, set up chairs in the formation you wish the players to sit. You should have chairs and music stands in place prior to the rehearsal. If you cannot provide music stands, let the instrumentalists know in advance so that they may bring their own stands to rehearsals or performances. Most instrumentalists own a portable wire stand and carry it in their case. You will want to find good chairs for the instrumentalists to sit for both the rehearsals and performances. Some players like to bring cushions, as some chairs can get hard over a long period of time. The chairs used for both choir and orchestra that are made by the Wenger Corporation are made just for this type of work. (Wenger 12-15).

As the people arrive for rehearsal, indicate where they are to sit. You could make a seating chart and post it on the bulletin board, or you could label chairs with the name of the player or the instrument they play. This is another good job for your assistant. You might want to provide space for instrument cases to be placed, especially if the performing area is cramped. Allow time for tuning and warm-up, and then proceed to get as much of the show rehearsed in the allotted time period. A two to three hour rehearsal should yield at least the reading of the first act, if not more. As the rehearsal is progressing, check for places where the instruments have rests, or tacets, so that at the next rehearsal you can have them fill music in from another book, if you are not using the full instrumentation. Allow the first rehearsal to be spent getting a feel for the music, the right notes, and correct tempi. You might be frustrated to learn that much of the first rehearsal is spent discovering mistakes in the various instrumental parts, and you might have to deal with incorrectly or poorly written notation. This is common. Rarely will one find a musical where the instrumental parts are totally devoid of error. Try to make these corrections quickly so that you can spend time on the performance of the music.

If your rehearsal period is two to three hours, be sure to schedule a five to ten minute break sometime after the first hour of work. Some people rehearse the overture and entr'acte and bow music after the break because these items contain music from all the songs in the show. They also are good items to rehearse to restore focus to the rehearsal following a break period.

I like to begin the first rehearsal with a couple of sentences of introduction to the musical prior to the first downbeat. Since not everyone knows the musical they are about to play, a few words such as, "This is a '40s show, which starred Ethel Merman," or "This is a contemporary show based on a Biblical story," or "This is one of my favorite shows, and I think you'll love the jazz element" will set the tone for the work session.

With instrumental rehearsals, as opposed to vocal rehearsals, it is probably best to start with the overture, and progress from one number to the next. There will be places where the strings and the woodwinds only play, such as in a ballad, and the brass and percussion may be tacet. Not every one plays in all movements. As you move from one number to another, you might even want to give a clue about each number to be rehearsed by saying: "This is the ballad," or "This is the love duet of the show," or "This is the big dance number." If you are not ashamed of your singing voice, you can sing along with the orchestra to give them a feel for the music they are playing.

To prepare the orchestra for what takes place before they play, you can set up a number with the dialog cue that will be said by the actors on stage just before the music begins. Some players will want to take the time to write this in their part. The conductor can even say these lines just before giving the preparatory gesture to the downbeat to reinforce the importance of the verbal cue. Not all music begins with verbal cues. If this is the case, you can inform the orchestra that the cue to begin will be a visual cue or action on stage which will determine when you give the downbeat. This will be helpful, especially if there are long passages of dialog between musical numbers.

At the second rehearsal, plan to get through the second act so that you will have read through the entire show in two rehearsals. If you are lucky, perhaps you can get through the music of the entire show in both rehearsals. If you are repeating music performed at the first rehearsal, be concerned with dynamics and places where certain nuances are required. Some actor/singers might wish to come to an instrumental rehearsal, and this is to be permitted, but they should understand that your primary interest is the instrumentalists, not the actors.

For young players, two or three rehearsals may not be sufficient before moving to dress rehearsals on stage. The number of instrumental rehearsals required will be based on the ability of the musicians available as well as the time schedule. With younger and inexperienced players, it may be necessary to have two weeks of rehearsals. Whatever is necessary, be sure to plan far enough in advance to allow for sufficient time to learn the music before dress rehearsal time.

It is nice if your final rehearsal with the orchestra could be what is known in German as a *Sitzprobe* or a "seated rehearsal." This rehearsal is when the music for the entire show is run for all cast members and orchestra. When time permits, this type of rehearsal is an excellent idea and makes the first rehearsal on-stage go much more smoothly. The *Sitzprobe* could be the first time that the cast members will hear the orchestra, as well as the first time the orchestra hears the singers. "This rehearsal is entirely geared towards the music, and the performers will not be required to dance, or to move" (White 107). Probably the only dialogue will be that for musical underscoring or to give musical cues. Most instrumental problems can be ironed out in two or three orchestra rehearsals so that you are ready for the first full-staged rehearsal when instrumentalists, actors, singers, set, and lights all work together for the first time.

If there is to be a *Sitzprobe*, the musical director will need to determine if this can be held with the actors on the stage and the instrumentalists in the orchestra pit. If the stage is being used for set construction and therefore not available, another location will need to be found. Perhaps the same room where the orchestra has been having their rehearsals is available. But, is it large enough to seat the entire cast as well as the orchestra? If the *Sitzprobe* is in a different location, the musical director will need to arrange for chairs for the cast as well as chairs and music stands for the instrumentalists. When we have a *Sitzprobe* that is not in the orchestra pit, the instrumentalists bring their own music stands. Wire stands are not always satisfactory because the part books do not always sit well on them. If this rehearsal site does not have its own percussion equipment, I do not require the percussionists to set up the full battery of equipment needed for the show. Often a bass drum and snare drum along with a cymbal are sufficient to keep the beat and provide the right effects.

Most choral directors who become involved in this sort of business are not prepared to discuss specific problems with instrumentalists. When a choral director addresses a musical problem to the choir, he refers to page numbers, staff system and measures, and deals with a text and notes. He and the choir are working from the same page of music which they all see. An instrumentalist has only his individual part and he sees nothing else. And, each instrumental part is different. Only the conductor has the full score. And remember, in musicals, there is only a piano/vocal score, not a partitur. Therefore, when the musical director addresses or gives instructions to instrumentalists, it is imperative that they know exactly where in the music you are when a particular concern is addressed. Therefore, be sure to give the number and/or title of the selection in question, then the measure number, then the beat of the measure, in that order. You would say, "In #19, 'Beach Journey Rock,' measure 14, beat 3, trumpets, give me a stronger accent." When you are addressing note issues, you would indicate the place in the score as above: number and title of the section, the measure number, the beat in the measure and then the specific note in question. When discussing notes, the instrumentalist will need to know if you are speaking of concert pitch or written pitch. In some cases these notes will be the same, but in many instances they will be different. An example of this will be, "At measure 5, do you have a Concert F or Concert G?" Or, you could say, "Instead of a Written G, play a Written F," depending upon the instrument in question and its transposition.

Not everyone is comfortable dealing with transposing instruments. For years, I have jokingly stated to the orchestra that, "I don't do windows, and I don't transpose!" This puts the onus on the instrumentalists to translate the notes in question into concert pitches. Rest assured that this conductor does understand transposition, but it was something that did not come naturally. It has required study on my part and I will confess that I need to refresh my mind now and then. Anyone working in the capacity of a musical director must have some knowledge of transposition should the novice player be transposing incorrectly or not know the difference! I will never forget working with a senior clarinet performance major, a fine musician and an experienced pit player. I asked him to add a 16 measure solo to his part from another instrumental book, which was written in concert pitch. He agreed to do it and at the next rehearsal announced he was prepared. But, when it came time for him to play, it sounded horrible! He had transposed the part one step up instead of one step down. He should have known better. On the other hand, as the musical director, it was my responsibility to provide the instrumentalist with the correct part to play or to make sure he knew how to do it correctly! Valuable lesson learned.

May I pass on some advice that was shared with me by a musician who had considerable professional experience in major symphonic orchestras as well as pit ensembles in Washington, D.C. and New York City. His words have served me well. Choral conductors are accustomed to having singers make marks in their music almost at the same time they are singing. My friend's advice was that when an instrumentalist needs to make a mark in his part, he must put down his instrument, pick up the pencil, make the mark, put down the pencil, pick up the instrument again before being ready to play. Instrumentalists need a little more time to make these marks. Many choral directors interpret these actions as a time consuming delay rather than understanding the situation. He also pointed out that most instrumentalists want to do a good job for the conductor, as they want to be hired and work for you again. I found this hint very helpful.

One last suggestion. The first technical or dress rehearsal in which the orchestra plays with the cast will run more smoothly if the musicians have some knowledge as to what the show is all about. This is especially true if the pit is situated so that the instrumentalists cannot see the stage. Some musical directors require the orchestra to read the script before the first music rehearsal. Another introduction to what is going on would be to have the musicians attend one of the final piano rehearsals so that they can see the cast perform the show, and run the dances while using only the piano accompaniment. Ask the instrumentalists to bring their music and follow along in their part while watching the rehearsal. This allows the musicians to see the show—especially watching the dance numbers—something they usually do not have a chance to do—and to discover how their music fits into the entire production. At the first technical rehearsal, they will be able to work without trying to crane their necks to see what is taking place on stage. This does not exclude the fact that orchestra will want to see the costumes the cast wears!

Another solution would be to have the first run-through with the orchestra in the cast's rehearsal space and have the instrumentalists fit in as best they can. Again, this will allow them to see much of the show and have a better feel for what is taking place. It also allows the actors to hear the orchestra before they begin dress rehearsals on the stage. Most instrumentalists who have a great deal of pit experience and have never seen the shows they have played. It is a shame that this is the case. But, that's the way it goes!

A word of confession. My first experience working with instrumentalists was conducting a choral piece which used two oboes and continuo. I was awed by these people who entered the room, opened their cases, put together their instruments, saw the music, and played it perfectly. Well, maybe not perfectly, but played it almost as well as the singers who had been rehearsing the music for several weeks. "Instrumentalists can do no wrong," I thought. Later, I came to learn that instrumentalists make mistakes, can have faulty pitch, and need correction just as choristers. Through rehearsal their performance improves. My experience working with instrumentalists has expanded my appreciation for music and I am grateful for this opportunity to learn from them.

After all the discussion about poorly written conductor's scores, illegible instrumental parts, handwritten chorus books and the like, this paragraph will come as a welcome surprise. Thanks to computer technology and the desire of some licensing agencies to supply error-free music, a new era is dawning for the world of the Broadway musical. Music Theatre International has developed two fantastic aids for use in the world of musical theatre. The first is called RehearScore. This is the program of the complete piano/vocal score played by a professional Broadway pianist which is to be used on a computer. Here, on a CD, are the complete dance numbers for the choreographer, as well as accompaniment for all the solo and chorus numbers. At this writing, there are forty-five titles available of the more popular shows, and more are being scheduled to be put into this format.

The second important announcement is that Music Theatre International is only one among several licensing agencies that is attempting to improve the quality and accuracy of the core holdings in their catalogs by republishing the piano/vocal score and the instrumental parts in legible format created by the use of computer music programs. In a recent performance of *Once Upon a Mattress,* all the orchestra parts had been reprinted, were legible, and virtually error free. This was a welcome change to the music rented in 1987 when I last conducted the show. Compare the 1957 page of "76 Trombones" from *The Music Man* with the same page which is currently available to observe the difference (see Example 23-1). Computer programs such as Finale and Sibelius have made it possible to have readable and accurate music. The only problem that I have found with these publications, other than the few notation errors, is that sometimes the part books do not lie flat on the stand causing some difficulty in reading the music near the binding because the pages tend to roll. Some agencies use spiral binding which allows the music to lie flat, but the plastic tends to break. I am sure a solution to this problem will be found soon.

Music Theatre International is taking this technology one step further! As mentioned earlier, it is not customary to have a partitur or full orchestral score available for musicals, even thought it would certainly be nice. MTI is now attempting to rectify this situation by making the option available. At this writing, there are sixteen shows which have a full orchestral scores available. And, MTI is providing Transpositions on Demand. Once the musical director and the soloist have decided the best key to sing a particular number(s) in the show in order to avoid the high (or low) notes that just are not there, one can "fill out the order form and send it to MTI along with your full payment. We'll send you the transposed piano/conductor part in just two days, and the required orchestra parts in about two weeks. We'll ship your transpositions unbound on individual sheets so you can insert them into your existing parts" (Music Theatre International 1997, 30). This is a wonderful service and is one example of how the computer age is making its impact felt to change and improve the music industry!

The original 1957 piano/conductor score for The Music Man.

MTI Times, winter 1997, p. 24. (Reprinted by permission from Music Theatre International.)

The Finale piano/conductor score for The Music Man.

Example 23-1. Comparison of Handwritten and Computer Generated Scores

Chapter 24

Conducting

This is not the place to spend a great deal of time talking about conducting technique or beat patterns. It is assumed that you have had conducting classes in college and some experience in conducting choirs. You may have had some instrumental work. Of all the qualities a conductor should possess to work successfully in a pit, I feel the most important should be clarity. Much of the music will be in simple patterns: 2/4, 3/4, and 4/4; the "two" pattern will be used frequently for both 2/4 as well as 6/8. There will be places where the conductor will need to show every beat of a 6/8; or even subdivide any of the other simple patterns. There will be some very fast places that will fall into a "one to the bar" pattern. You should be equally comfortable showing 5/8 or 7/8 patterns or other uneven meters as more contemporary musicals commonly use mixed meters. If all of the patterns mentioned above, as well as all cueing gestures, are clear and precise, if they convey the mood, dynamic level, and tempo, then the majority of your conducting problems are solved.

Giving cues to instrumentalists is not always possible in the early rehearsal stages, as the piano/vocal score does not always tell which instrument is playing a particular musical line. But, one can look at the trumpet section when the score indicates trumpets and after one or two rehearsals, you will know if that means all the trumpets in the section or only Trumpet I. Cues will need to be given to actors on stage as well as to the chorus. In rehearsals, they will depend on these more than they will toward the end of the run, but they will be counting on you at all times.

Giving cues to actors on stage is usually indicated with the cue hand, most commonly the left hand. A strong pointing gesture to the actor when it is time to sing is usually all that is required (see Example 24-1).

You should be comfortable, however, giving cue gestures with the cue hand as well as with the baton hand. I recall attending a Broadway production where

Example 24-1. Giving a Cue

the actor needed help knowing when to sing as well as when not to sing. The conductor solved this problem by pointing when to sing, and holding up his hand like a policeman stopping traffic indicating when not to sing. More than likely, you will only need to show your singers when to sing. The only stopping indication will be a strong cutoff at the end of the piece.

A baton must always be used when conducting in a pit, whether or not you like to use one, or whether you have ever used one in your other conducting experiences. You will save yourself a lot of physical energy, your gestures will be more clear, and you will be less fatigued at the end of the performance if a baton is used. Your instrumentalists will be able to follow you much better, as many of them will be sitting to your side rather than all sitting to your front. Also, most of the instrumentalists who have performed in orchestras and bands are accustomed to seeing a baton. And, your performers on stage can follow better, too. (Plus, a baton makes a wonderful back scratcher for those hard to reach places!)

Many conductors who are not accustomed to using a baton make the mistake of holding the baton incorrectly. They hold it in such a way that the baton points to the ceiling of the theatre rather than to the stage, or to the orchestra. The baton must be held so that it works as an extension of your arm and points to the proper area: to the stage, or to the orchestra, not the ceiling (see Examples 24-2 and 24-3).

Example 24-2. Correct Position

Example 24-3. Incorrect Position

Should you stand or sit to conduct? The answer is probably that you should be in a position to be seen easily by the actors and the orchestra, that you should be in a position that is comfortable for you, and you should be as unobtrusive to the audience as possible. I have been in situations where it was necessary to sit while conducting since the pit was not deep enough to allow me to stand. And, I learned to be comfortable conducting in a seated position. However, I prefer to conduct standing.

Getting the music started is the primary job of any conductor, and it is certainly a major concern for the musical theatre conductor. One starts the overture. Then you start a number after some dialogue has been spoken. Then you must start the music from a visual cue from the stage. Then you start dance numbers. Or you change tempi in the middle of a number. It seems the conductor is always starting! Of course, it goes without saying that the conductor must always start the music in the correct tempo for the singers, for the dancers, as well as for the mood/tempo of the show. It is a very responsible job!

Not all instrumentalists in your orchestra will have worked with singers or played in pits previously. They may have done most of their playing in halftime shows for football games, or playing for a rock concert. You will need to educate them that in musicals, one plays under the singers, but the orchestra always supports the singers and the action on stage. The statement, "A good orchestra is not merely accompaniment, but also enhances the action by providing subliminal clues to character and mood" (Rosewell 1981, 53) is another way of illustrating this support that is necessary for any production. This does not mean that the orchestra is "subservient to the singers. The art of playing softly yet with intensity and the ability to change dynamic levels according to the action on stage will need to be rehearsed" (Rosewell 1981, 53). This statement illustrates how important the orchestra's job really is! And you, the musical director, are the person responsible for all this.

Not every number in a show supports singers. There are always dance numbers, overtures, and playoffs where the orchestra does not have to worry about covering up the voices on stage. I have coined a phrase that I share with my players, whether they are accompanying the singers or playing for a big dance number: "When in doubt, play half as loud, twice as rhythmic." To me, it makes a great deal of sense. It is the rhythmic drive that makes the music soar and the audience tap their toes! At the same time, it tells the orchestra that they are not to play so loudly that it is just noise! Usually the instrumentalists need to mark their parts down at least one dynamic level in order to achieve the proper balance between pit and stage. If they still play as rhythmically as possible, they will give the necessary support to action on stage and give a tremendous vitality to the production.

Urge the instrumentalists to listen to what is taking place on the stage. If they learn the show as they play, they will be alert should problems arise, such as when a singer misses a cue, skips a beat, or flubs words. Music theatre history books could be written on how an alert orchestra has saved a performance from disaster by knowing the show so well that they were able to jump a beat or two, or even a measure or two to the right spot. And, this all takes place within a fraction of a second . . . much to the relief of the conductor!

A conductor must always be involved in the music—what is going on in the pit, as well as what is taking place on stage—and at the same time be able to step back and try to observe the performance as if he were a person in the audience. In this way the conductor will be aware of volume . . . perhaps the most common flaw of amateur musical theatre orchestras. They tend to play too loudly. Remind your orchestra that the audience usually does not make any comment about the orchestra unless they play so loudly that they overpower the singers. It will probably come as a revelation to the instrumentalists that as important as they are to the success of the show, the most important element for the theatre-goer is being able to understand the words. Engel has summed it so beautifully when he states

> The most important aspect to remember is the relationship between the voices to be heard from the stage and the instrumental sounds from the pit. No matter what adjustment is required—whether because the voices are small or the acoustics bad—no matter, not a single word or lyric should be sacrificed to any orchestral sound. (Engel 1966, 83)

If the conductor has the privilege of having an assistant conductor, use this person to take one of the rehearsals so that you can sit out in the theatre. This will give you a totally different perspective to the show. You will be viewing it as a member of the audience, and you will learn a great deal. You will be able to determine the balance between the orchestra and the singers on stage. You will be able to hear the orchestra much better and can tell if certain solo instrumental lines are being drowned out by other instrumentalists. I always found that the sound I heard being played by the bass in the orchestra pit did not seem to be as loud as it did to the patrons out in the audience. I do not always have the luxury of an assistant, but when I do, I try and take advantage of observing a rehearsal from the viewer's perspective.

Chapter 25

Pit Placement of Instrumentalists

Assuming the production takes place in a theatre, obviously the instrumentalists sit in the orchestra pit. It is easy to understand how the name "pit orchestra" is given to the accompanying ensemble. What is the best way to arrange the instrumentalists? Since orchestra pits in theatres differ in size and depth, the set up used for the production will vary greatly. Example 25-1 shows a fairly common arrangement.

In this setup, the drum-set is at the back of the pit, directly in front of the conductor along with the bass. If a guitar is used, it should be seated with these rhythm players. This allows for the rhythm to be in the center of the ensemble as well as directly in front of the conductor so that tempi can be solidly maintained. The strings (violins, violas) would be to the conductors left, sitting two to a stand facing the right wall of the auditorium. The cello(s) can be placed

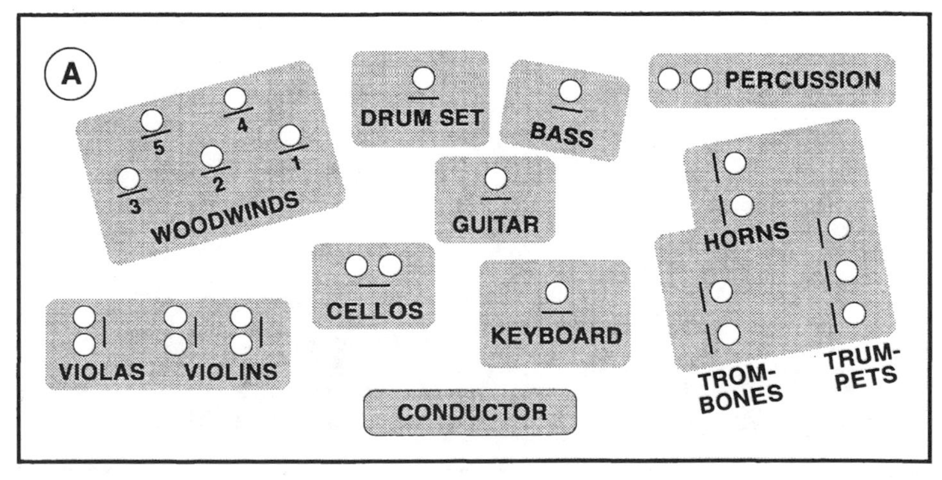

Example 25-1. Suggested Pit Arrangement A

directly in front of the conductor, facing the audience in order to assure good projection. If space permits, another place for the cellos would be behind the violins and violas. The brass (trumpets, trombones, horns) to the conductor's right, facing the left wall of the auditorium. It may be necessary to place a baffle in front of the trumpets to help with balance. This could be a heavy cloth curtain hung behind the music stands. It could even be a Plexiglas panel which mutes the sound, but is clear so that the players can see the conductor. Whether you place the trumpets in front of the trombones or behind them may be a question of space and conductor's preference. One needs to be sure that all the instruments have sufficient playing space: the strings need room for comfortable bowing, the brass need room for the various mutes they use, and the trombones sufficient space for their slides. Let us assume there will be at least five woodwinds and they are doublers. They will need space for the multiple instruments they are required to play so that they can smoothly transfer from one to the other with ease.

If a piano is used (either electric or acoustic) it might be placed at the back of the pit with rhythm instruments or near the front of the pit. Arrangement B (Example 25-2) is similar to arrangement A, but it indicates the placement when two percussionists are required. The drum-set will be placed against the house right wall facing the conductor with the remainder of the area behind the instruments used for the other percussionist playing orchestra bells, xylophone, marimba, and timpani. In this arrangement, the piano is placed near the front of the pit or behind the woodwinds. It will be noted that the piano and the percussion would work equally well in either of the places indicated.

More contemporary shows are written with one or more synthesizers required to create the various sounds the composer needs. These multi-keyboards

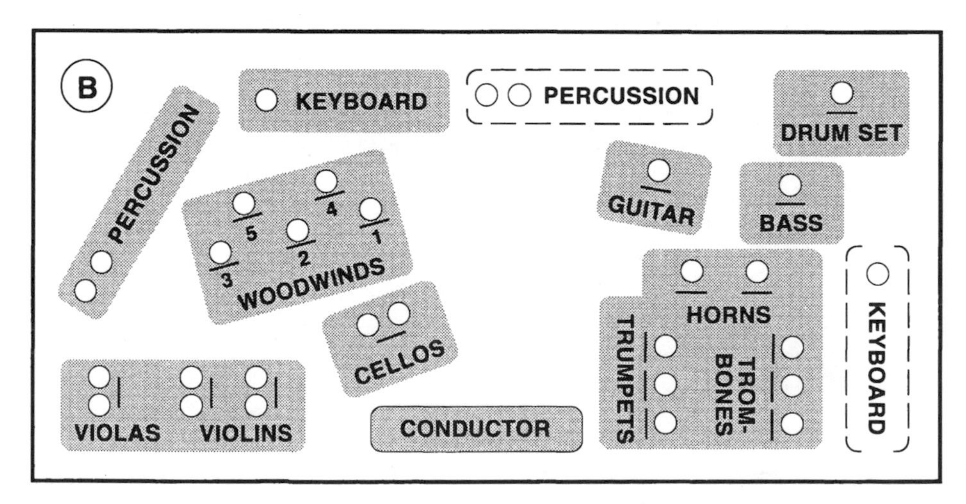

Example 25-2. Suggested Pit Arrangement B

can be placed directly in front of the conductor as shown by arrangement C (see Example 25-3).

These pit arrangement diagrams are merely suggestions. Orchestra pits are notoriously small and crowded. One writer suggests that, "Office workers would not put up with a workstation where they had to sit hunched or twisted to fit into a few square feet of space allotted to them, but pit musicians often tolerate this as 'part of the job'" (Paull and Harrison 156). They continue their discussion on the "Perils of the Pit" with a warning that in addition to lack of space, the orchestra pit can be the receiver of objects that are intended for use on stage. It is not uncommon to find professional theatres placing safety-netting over the orchestra to avoid accidents (Paull and Harrison 156).

The illustrations for pit set up provided here give a false sense of spaciousness that does not really exist. You will have to adjust your set up plan to the space you have available and the instruments being used. Whatever your space allocation, you will find it beneficial to group families of instruments together: e.g. the woodwinds together, the brass together, etc. Be sure to place whatever instruments that make up the rhythm section, the drum set, the bass, and the guitar as a group. This will assure a solid rhythmic drive for the ensemble.

The use of a piano in the pit, even when it is not called for in the score, can be a helpful tool for performance. In some theatres, it is difficult for the actors to hear the orchestra, especially during big dance numbers. Placing a microphone in the piano and connecting it to speakers placed in the wings of the stage can serve as a rhythmic support for the performers. Again, the physical set up will vary greatly and this may not be a necessity in your performance space.

The electrical needs for the musicians are a very important factor for consideration. Each music stand must have its own individual light. (Some

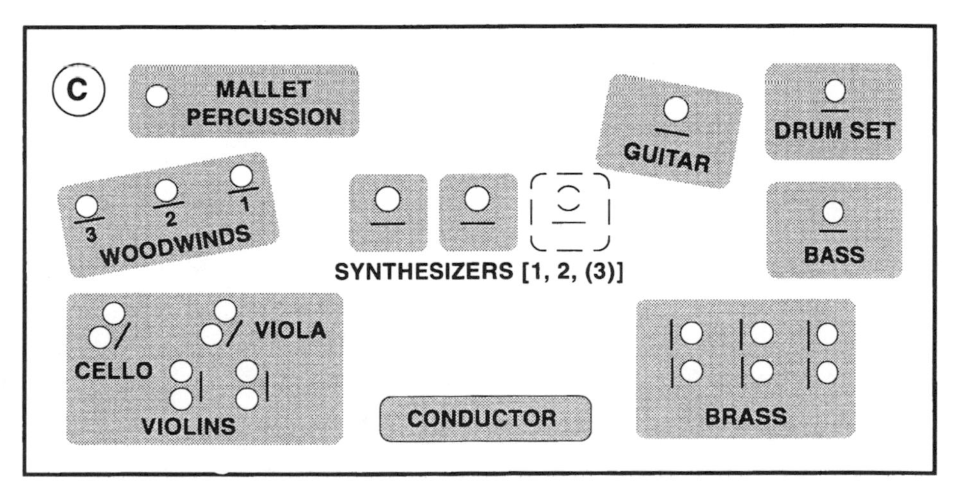

Example 25-3. Suggested Pit Arrangement C

instrumentalists prefer to use two lights on their stand, as this spreads light more evenly over the entire score.) If electric guitar, electric bass, or synthesizers are used, these instruments will require additional outlets. Few pits are equipped with sufficient electrical plugs to meet these requirements, so it will be necessary to run extension cords and electrical strips so everyone can plug in. Setting up the pit and arranging for its electrical demands is another excellent job for the pit manager.

Some musical productions take place in buildings that were never intended for theatrical productions, such as an auditorium which was designed for concerts, not theatrical productions. Some of these locations will not even have an orchestra pit. Or, the pit will be less than adequate—being either too shallow and not sufficiently deep to allow the orchestra to be out of sight of the audience, or the pit could be so deep that it is impossible for the conductor to see the stage if he stands on the same level as the instrumentalists. Some productions will take place in buildings that have no orchestra pit at all, such as a gymnasium. In these cases, the instrumental ensemble should be off to one side, out of the sight-line of the audience. There are some productions that have the orchestra on the stage with the cast as in *The Robber Bridegroom* or *Chicago*. In others, the orchestra may be placed behind the stage and it is necessary to use closed-circuit television for the conductor to see the action on stage.

Regardless of the physical setup of your particular production, the people on stage must be able to hear the orchestra. The conductor must be able to see the stage in order to coordinate the action on stage with the instrumentalists. And, in every case, the orchestra should be as unobtrusive as possible. Be creative!

Chapter 26

Vamp

You have rehearsed everyone. You know how to arrange the instrumentalists in the space allowed. You are comfortable with the beat patterns and other conducting gestures. Now we deal with specific conducting situations in the score. The most commonly used musical device used in Broadway productions is the vamp. A vamp, sometimes called a "safety," is a one measure (sometimes two-measure) passage which can be repeated over and over, either at the beginning or somewhere in the middle of a song.[13] A vamp is a great help should actors not be in place when it is time to begin a number, or if more time is needed before continuing the rest of the song, or for covering some stage business, or there is some dialog to be said over an underscoring. A vamp allows for the actors to hold for a moment should there be audience reaction and the actor must hold for laughter or applause before continuing. There is no set time for how many times a vamp measure is repeated. During the vamp, the orchestra is in a state of suspended animation until whatever is happening on stage is ready to move on to the next action. It is also a way of giving the singer the pitch and tempo of a song. "Vamp till ready" has been a standard motto in the theatre for years as well as a part of the jargon for various walks of life. Vamps vary in length from performance to performance. That is their purpose—to allow for the orchestra to be in neutral before shifting into gear and continue playing. "When used well, it is one of the most valuable of all practical devices that appears in the score" (Grote 49).

Vamps are well-marked in the music, usually by the standard repeat signs surrounding the measure, with the word "vamp" written above the measure as shown in Example 26-1. In the example from a passage of *Beach Journey*, Joe has just sung the phrase ending with the words, "love you." There is a short passage of dialog, during which the orchestra is playing the vamp measure. The conductor holds the orchestra in vamp until he hears Mary say the words, "check the map." Joe will have been listening to the orchestra and will know when to

Example 26-1. Musical Example of a Vamp from *Beach Journey*

continue singing with the words, "And we will go . . ." Until Joe begins singing, the orchestra continues playing the vamp measure or is in "neutral." On signal, orchestra and singer will move on.

It is sometimes necessary to create a vamp where more time is needed for stage business. The musical director can do this by deciding that a particular passage is to be repeated until the stage business or dialog is completed. To create a vamp, select a measure or measures that can be played more than once with ease and which make musical sense if repeated. Have the instrumentalists mark this passage with repeat marks on both sides of the measure(s), and treat this section as a vamp in the same manner as any other vamp found in the score.

In a recent a production of *Sweet Charity*, we found that the music indicated was not long enough to cover both action on the stage as well as dialog. The decision was made to create a vamp to cover this. The orchestra marked their scores making measures 6A and 6B into a vamp (see Example 26-2). This solved the problem. This inserted vamp was played two or three times in order do whatever was necessary on stage, and did not leave a dead-space in the scene. Warning! If you find that you are playing any vamp more than two or three times, this might be a clue that you need to look for different music to cover the scene change. Nothing will alert the audience that something is taking longer than necessary more than hearing the same music played incessantly!

Often times, these created vamps may be necessary in rehearsals, but once into production they are no longer needed because the pace of things has quickened. If they are no longer needed, indicate this to the orchestra and have them change their scores. However, the reverse can be equally true. Due to a difference in performance space or of audience reaction more time may be needed.

Example 26-2.
Musical Example of a Created Vamp
from "Where Am I Going" from *Sweet Charity.*
(used by permission)

Some scene change music is rather brief. In these instances, the last measure(s) could be indicated in the score as a vamp. Should the stage crew not do their job quickly enough, the orchestra is stuck in a vamp until the lights come up on the next scene. Another saying, "Never let the orchestra vamp," is a rule for the stage crew to encourage them to do their job quickly so that the audience's attention is not diverted from the action of the show.

As musical director, you will not be responsible or even concerned about the shifting of scenery or other back stage activities. But it is your job to see that there is sufficient music to cover these activities. You will hope that everything that takes place back stage goes smoothly and quickly. Boland and Argentini caution against having scenery that is so bulky or complicated that it will prevent these changes from taking place effortlessly. No audience wants to sit in the dark waiting for the next scene to take place. "A good rule is that all scenery changes must be accomplished in less than one minute," suggest Boland and Argentini. Shorter would be seen as better "In the professional theatre the limit is thirty seconds." (Boland and Argentini 1997, 7).

As the conductor, you *must* be able to indicate clearly when the ensemble is in the vamp and when it is time to move out of the vamp. A simple hand signal is all that is necessary. The raising of the index finger of the non-baton hand is the standard cue for indicating a vamp, whether you are in a professional theatre in New York City or in your local high school amateur production. When going into the vamp, hold up the index finger of the non-baton hand. Since some people use their left hand for conducting, I am not indicating which is the cue hand. Hold your hand at face level or so that your raised finger can be easily seen by the entire orchestra. As long as you are in the vamp, remain in that position, keeping the beat going with the baton hand, using a small pattern as shown in Example 26-3.

Example 26-3. Left Hand Position for Vamp

When you need to move out of the vamp, drop your cue hand and use a slightly larger gesture with the baton hand. The orchestra will finish playing the vamp measure, move to the following measure and continue playing the rest of the selection. In the example from "Where am I Going" from *Sweet Charity* (Example 26-2), the conductor should indicate to the orchestra that they are in vamp at the beginning of measure 6A by raising the finger of his non-baton hand. The orchestra would repeat measures 6A and 6B until they receive the indication they are released from vamp. When the conductor hears the actor say the speech which ends, "I don't know where," he knows the music can continue. If these words are spoken near the beginning of the vamp, he would drop his cue hand which indicates to the orchestra that at the end of measure 6-B they should continue to measures 7. By giving a slightly larger preparation into the down beat as they cross the bar line, he is assured that all of the orchestra will move together.

If the actor's cue comes too near the end of measure 6B, an instantaneous decision must be made. Can the orchestra react quickly enough to move into measure 7, or is it better to continue holding the orchestra for one more repeat of the vamp before continuing to measure 7? This is where experience determines the decision. If you have seasoned players who react quickly, it might be safe to get out of the vamp and continue. With less experienced players or with an orchestra not familiar with the show, it might be better to play it safe. By not dropping your non-baton hand, the orchestra will remain in vamp, thus playing it one more time before you indicate for them to move on. This assumes, however, that the actor on stage doesn't jump into the next phrase of the song because he has said the cue line. The actor should wait for a cuc from the conductor anyway. This is just another example of how alert a conductor needs to be at all times in order to cue players in the pit as well as the actors on the stage.

It is imperative that you practice getting in and out of vamps just as you would any other conducting gesture. It is one that is frequently used, and it is absolutely necessary that it be indicated smoothly and clearly. You will save yourself many serious headaches if you are comfortable doing this and your orchestra has confidence in your ability to show it.

There are many stories about conductors and vamps. One of them tells of a professional conductor who had trouble indicating getting out of a vamp. His solution for this inability was to tell the orchestra, "When you hear the singer, it is time to move on." This is only part of the solution! It *is* helpful to tell the orchestra that when the singer begins to sing, or sings a certain word, we are out of the vamp. This is especially true if there is a pick-up to the vocal line which is in the last half of the vamp measure. However, this does not eliminate the conductor's responsibility that clarity is absolutely mandatory! Another vamp story concerns a different professional conductor working with a professional orchestra in a major city. This conductor's indications for vamps were so unclear that the members of the orchestra were forced to agree among themselves how to get in and out of the vamp, thus saving the production from disaster.

Some scores will have places that call for "double vamps." In this situation, there are two measures in succession and each measure is a separate vamp. Your problem is to be able to indicate to the orchestra when they are to move from the first vamp measure to the second vamp measure. In both cases the cue to move the orchestra is either a visual or a word cue.

A well-known example of a double vamp can be found in "Two Lost Souls" from *Damn Yankees*. To clearly indicate to the orchestra where we were, the cue for the first vamp was shown with the customary index finger gesture. This vamp was held until the sight-cue told the conductor that it was time to move on to the second vamp. Here a larger down-beat was used to indicate a shift to the next measure and the conductor extended both the index finger as well as the little finger to indicate the second vamp. This gesture was held while continuing to beat with a small pattern. One could have indicated the second vamp by using the first and second fingers on the cue hand just as well. The second vamp was held until the actors had completed their stage business and were ready to move on with the song. When the singers began to sing, the conductor dropped the cue hand, used a larger gesture with the baton hand, and the number continued.

The example of a double vamp from *Beach Journey* (Example 26-4) is similar to the one described from *Damn Yankees*. The second measure of the example is the first vamp and would be indicated with the index finger. This

Example 26-4.
Musical Example of a Double Vamp from *Beach Journey*

measure is repeated until the actor says, "Well! You order." This is the cue to move into the second vamp.

The conductor would indicate to the orchestra that they move to the second vamp by holding two fingers (Example 26-5). The orchestra knows they should be in the second vamp and they will play this until the conductor sees the actor playing the part of John stand. This visual action from the stage is the conductor's cue to drop his non-baton hand, use a larger down beat indicating to the orchestra that they are now out of the second vamp. They respond by moving to the next measure of music and will continue with the remainder of the selection.

Vamps are not to be confused with repeats. You will find that the score will sometimes have several measures enclosed in repeat bars. During rehearsals you will have decided if the repeat is to be played through and ignored; if the repeat is to be repeated once; or if it is repeated more than once. The numbers of times it is repeated will be set in rehearsals. You will relay this information to the orchestra: whether the measures in the repeat signs are played through or if the repeat is observed. When it has been agreed how many times the repeat is taken, I usually indicate with my cue hand the number of times playing the repeat, just in case someone loses count. To help the orchestra in counting the number of times repeated, the conductor can indicate the first time played by indicating with one finger, on the second playing, holding up of two fingers, and showing three fingers on the third playing. Repeats are often found only in instrumental passages. Vamps are often in places leading into vocal passages or where specific action is needed on stage.

Example 26-5. Hand Position for Double Vamp

One may find that similar finger signals are needed to relay cues to the singers/dancers on the stage. In big production numbers that end with singing, or any type of situation where singers need to be cued when it is close to the time to sing, the conductor can count down the measures before their entry. As shown in Example 26-6, holding up four fingers just below one's chin when there are four measures before singing, then changing to three fingers, then to two fingers, and finally to one finger, is a way of helping the performers count down to their entrance. The chorus may need more assistance early in the production in being alerted to their entrance than later during the run. However, should they become too involved with the action on the stage during performance, the conductor's assistance will aid in a secure vocal entrance.

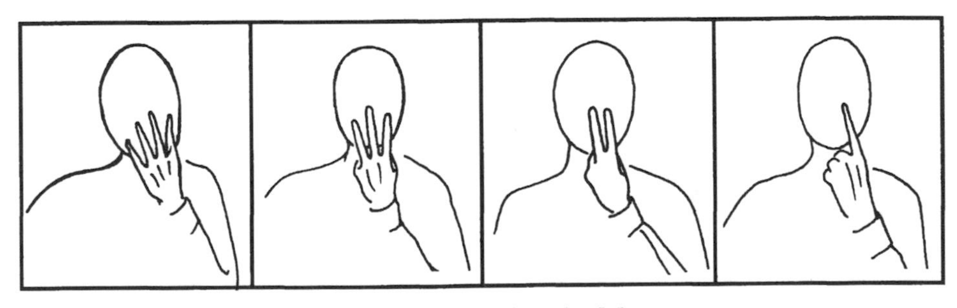

Example 26-6. Counting the Measures

Chapter 27

Holding It All Together: Transitions

Underscoring

There will be shows that call for music to be played under dialog. This is referred to as underscoring. This technique appears in many older shows, such as *Show Boat* as well as in contemporary works, such as *Tintypes* and *Children of Eden.* Regardless of the vintage of the show, the practice is the same. There is music to support the mood of the scene, and this music is to be played under the spoken dialog of the actors. There are some problems that you will encounter with underscoring. The most frequent one is that the orchestra will play too loudly and the dialog will not be heard or understood. Of course, the best solution is to ask the instrumentalists to play more softly. Playing very softly, without proper breath support, can result in poor sounds. Another solution would be to reduce the number of instrumentalists playing the underscoring. Maybe the solution would be to eliminate the woodwind parts and leave the strings, or the reverse. The brass are rarely asked to play in underscoring situations. Another solution would be to omit all instruments and use only the piano played softly. The last resort would be to cut the underscoring completely. When you are rehearsing the orchestra, it is a good idea to let them know that a particular passage is under dialog. This will alert them of the need to play softly. The orchestra will try their best to comply to your instructions, but sometimes the configuration and location of the pit is such that no matter how softly they play, it is still too loud.

Another problem with underscoring is when the dialog and the music need to reach the same place at the same time. Some piano/vocal scores will have certain passages of the dialog written above the music. This gives the conductor an idea if the underscoring needs to be played more slowly or more quickly.

There will sometimes be key places where the music and the text are to coincide. Regardless of what is written in the score, one must keep in mind that these cues may not work in your situation. The spoken cues in the music were for the original production in an environment different from where you are performing. This does not mean that coordination will be impossible. It does mean that the musical director needs to be familiar with the entire passage of dialog in order to try to move the music a little quicker or to slow it down in case it is crucial to the performance that the ending is together.

It has been my experience that it is sometimes necessary to build in a safety net in this type of music should things not be working out correctly. One safety could be for the instrumentalists to insert a *cesura* or "railroad tracks" somewhere in the underscoring should the music be ahead of the dialog. In this way, they can wait for a beat or two, then continue playing at a particular dialog passage on your cue. I find it is better to let the music come to a halt rather than slowing down to a ridiculously slow tempo to make every word try to come together with the music. By the same token, the actors may need to be told that it will help if they hold their dialog with some stage business until they hear a particular musical passage or receive a cue from the conductor.

Applause Segue

When a musical number takes place in the beginning or middle of a scene and dialog will follow the number, the performers often are "frozen" at the conclusion of the number for the applause before continuing with the dialog. Some scores contain an additional bit of music which is to be played in this space. This music is an applause segue. Sometimes this will be a few measures from the music just sung. The piano/vocal score will have the dialog cue printed in score. If not, the musical director will need to write this in the score if it is not there. The dialogue is the indication when the music should fade off and stop. Or, the cue to stop the music may be an action on stage or a visual act that will be the reason for stopping the music.

There are many times when an applause segue gets in the way of the action. If this is the case, it is best to omit the music. The reverse is equally true. If the director feels there should be some music after the song before the dialog, an applause segue can be created by playing the last four or eight measures of the music that has just been performed, making just the right tag to cover until the next stage action takes place. For example, in a production of *Cinderella*, there was a number which ended with the King, the Queen, and about ten male singer/dancers on stage. The next action in the script was dialogue between the King and Queen, but the dancers needed to be off the stage before this dialog began. To do this smoothly, the last eight measures of the music were repeated for the exit of the ten men. When the music stopped, the dialog continued.

Play-Off/Bridge

A play-off is similar to the applause segue and the terms could be used interchangeably. However, for all practical purposes the play-off is the music at the end of a number, a scene, or a dance number which ends the scene and is used to cover the exit of actors or the change of scenery into the next scene. "It could provide the transition back into the dramatic action, smoothing the way for continuity" (Berkson 34). In older musicals, the music for play-offs is written out. It is possible that you will find you need some music to serve as a play-off. If this is the case, it will need to be created.

In more modern shows, the scene changes are extremely rapid thanks to unit sets and mechanically controlled scenery that are common to the current Broadway stage. These changes take place so quickly there is rarely any need to use music to cover this action. Amateur productions will not have this type of technology and the scene changes will take a bit longer. The piano/vocal score may not provide any music to cover the applause or the scene change action. It will be your job as musical director to find something appropriate to fill this dead space. You can select passages from a dance number, from the overture and/or entr'acte. One of the easiest ways is to use the final measures of the number just completed. It will also save the orchestra from flipping pages to find the music for this purpose. Play-off music should try and capture the mood of the scene just finished, or prepare the mood for the forthcoming scene. In many cases, the music does not need to be written out by the orchestra. They can just make pencil notes to indicate which measures need to be played to cover this action. Once the play-off has been agreed upon, the orchestra plays this music after the number completed on the conductor's next cue. Likewise, the orchestra will stop on your cue should the lights come up before the play-off music is completed. Try and find play-off music that will avoid places where awkward page turns are involved. If there is no other solution, have the orchestra members copy these measures from the part books and insert it in the places needed.

Overture and Entr'acte

The orchestra is responsible for the music which begins the show, called the overture, as well as the music which starts the action of the second act, called the entr'acte. These musical items serve a major function, such as covering the arrival of late comers, setting the mood of the evening, and introducing the audience to music that is to be heard in the show. The length of overtures and entr'actes will vary. *Sound Of Music* begins with the tolling of a bell and goes instantly into the singing of the first number by the nuns, the *Dixit Dominus—Rex admirabilis—Alleluia*. Other shows, such as *Oklahoma* have an extended overture which plays through almost every tune in the entire show.

It is wonderful to hear the music in these longer overtures and entr'actes. Your instrumentalists will enjoy playing them because it is their time to shine. But, it might be necessary to consider the ability of the orchestra and the length of these pieces and come to a decision whether they add or detract from the overall pacing of the production. It is sometimes expedient to shorten these, especially the entr'acte music, so that the show can get started without too much delay. Another reason to shorten the overture will be the quality of the musicians in the pit, because playing the entire overture "is an easy way for the show to get off to a bad start. Many amateur orchestras are fine as a support to singers but lack the dexterity to perform a mini-concert by themselves" (Hustoles 392). When talent and ability warrants, it is my practice to play the entire overture, or as much of it as possible. Depending upon the length of the entr'acte music, I make the decision whether to play all of it or just a portion. Having a shorter entr'acte allows for the show to resume quickly following the intermission.

Bows

The score will contain the music for the orchestra to play at the end of the performance when the cast members take their curtain calls. This music is labeled as "bows" in the score. Sometimes it is a repeat of the final or closing number of the show. It could be a repeat of some of the more familiar musical items that occurred earlier in the production. It may be necessary for the orchestra to play this music more than once to cover the time required for the company to get on stage and take their bows.

Instead of repeating the bow music, you could move directly to the last item in the score, the exit music. Depending upon how much exit music is provided in the score, it may be necessary for the musical director to indicate where repeats should be made, should there not be enough music. Sometimes cuts need to be made if there is more music than needed for the cast to take their bows.

In some musicals, there could be places for the chorus and principals to sing or even dance during the bows. These "singing bows" frequently reprise the final number of the show, or one of the more popular songs. The wonderful Gershwin show, *Crazy For You*, not only has singing in the music for bows, but includes one more tap number for everyone to do. *Joseph and the Amazing Technicolor Dreamcoat* reprises almost the entire show in its bows section!

Exit Music

The final item the orchestra is responsible for is the exit music. The purpose of this music is to provide a reprise of the show's tunes as the audience leaves the theatre thus sending them on their way with a tune in their head. The contents of the exit music will vary. For some shows, this is a repeat of the overture, or of the entr'acte music. It may even be a repeat of the final number.

It could even be a medley of some of the tunes from the show. As musical director, you will need to decide if it is necessary to play all of the exit music provided in the score to cover the exit of the audience. You may need more music. You may need less music.

At the first performance, you may discover that you have too much music for the exit of the audience. If this is the case, see if there is a cut that can be made. If one can be easily done, ask the instrumentalists to note this in their parts. Rehearse the cut, and incorporate it at the next performance. If you need more music, reverse the process. Find a section that can be easily repeated, mark it, rehearse the change and incorporate this into the next performance.

There are some shows that have no exit music at all. If this is the case, it is necessary for the musical director to create some, unless the director would like the audience to leave the theatre without any music being played. To find some music to use, look through the score and find a fully orchestrated passage from a dance section, or a portion of the overture. If this seems to fit your need, use this for the exit music. At the instrumental rehearsal, indicate to the orchestra where the exit music is to come from and have the players make a note in their score where they are supposed to play.

In a recent production of *Grease,* the orchestra members did not find the exit music in the score to be too much fun to play. Instead, they agreed to jam in a twelve-bar Blues style until the majority of the audience had exited, much to the delight of the front row audience members. In a production of *Mikado*, the decision was made to omit the overture, due to its length, and begin the show with the opening number which had an extended instrumental introduction. Since Gilbert and Sullivan had provided no exit music at the end of the show, the last half of the overture was played as exit music. It worked perfectly.

I am always pleased when audience members remain in the house until the exit music is finished, just as I am pleased when members of the congregation stay to hear the organist's postlude at end of a church service. A young, inexperienced orchestra may feel that the exit music is not important, but they need to be informed that their job is not finished until the cut-off at the last note of the exit music. There will be people who stay to hear that very last note. And their applause at this time is always warmly received.

Chapter 28

That "Sticky" Question

"Does the orchestra follow the singers or the conductor?" is a question I am frequently asked. When everything is working as it should, one would hope that we do everything together and it comes out perfectly. But we all know that is not always true. The usual procedure should be that the conductor sets the tempo of the music in performance the same way it has been rehearsed with the singers and dancers in rehearsal. It is the musical director's responsibility to reconstruct this tempo every time. If the conductor finds this is difficult to do, it will be necessary to purchase an electronic metronome which can give the correct tempo. These are compact gadgets which can be set to give whatever tempo is indicated either with a clicking sound or the flashing of a light. One of these should be kept handy even in rehearsals for setting proper tempi.

In performances, I assume the attitude that there is some degree of give and take between cast and orchestra. As the conductor, I will attempt to recreate the agreed upon tempo of all numbers. I also know that once a number has been in performance several times a slightly quicker tempo becomes more comfortable for everyone. By contrast, I know that one night a soloist may take a little more liberty than normal just because of the magic of the moment, and if the orchestra plowed to the cadence without acknowledging this, it would ruin the effect. Flexibility under the guise of consistency is the rule.

But, what about mistakes that take place during a performance? Should such a train-wreck occur on stage, cross your fingers and try to keep going. If the actor has gone blank and cannot remember the right words, you can try and give the singer the word cue word by mouthing what should be sung. Most times the actors will sing some words, regardless of what they are, rather than resort to silence. The more frequent problem is that the actor will skip a beat in a measure, delete a beat of rest and come in early or late. Depending on whether the actor can clearly hear the orchestra, they will keep on singing thus being ahead or behind the music. It could be that you are one or two measures off. In these cases, it may be necessary for the conductor to call out a measure number to the orchestra, hope they can hear you and will jump to the correct place in the music. What seems like centuries is probably only one or two seconds at the most. While it may seem like the sinking of the *Titanic* to you, it is quite possible that the flaw will go unnoticed by the audience. There have been times, firmly etched in my memory, of little tragedies that have taken place in a performance. An alert orchestra has saved the day by jumping to the correct measure with the actor, and continuing on as if nothing had happened. This shift happened more quickly than it would have taken for the conductor to say where in the music they should skip. Alert pit musicians who know what is taking place in the pit as well as on stage are to be coveted! Just another example that pit playing is not hack-work and requires alert, talented, competent musicians.

Can one prepare the orchestra for these performance emergencies? Yes and no. Since you can never predict when and where they will take place, it is impossible to announce the tragedy in advance! But you can continually urge the orchestra to be alert to what is taking place on stage. One could even find that "rehearsing the orchestra for the possibility of mishaps—speeding or slowing the tempo instantaneously, or skipping beats and measures when necessary" (Rosewell 1981, 53) will prepare them for the eventuality of a performance flaw. One way of keeping the orchestra alert, is to change the tempo of places that will not affect the cast. You could perform sections in the overture slightly faster or slower, hold a fermata one beat longer than normal, and not affect the overall performance. But, a slight alteration keeps everyone on their toes. I attended a professional performance where a friend was a member of the orchestra. When we visited at intermission, I commented on how tightly the orchestra was playing. "We have never performed this show with this conductor," was my friend's reply. "The adrenaline is really pumping" (Bunn 1998). It seems that the regular conductor was ill, and the assistant was conducting this performance. Everyone was alert, cast and orchestra, because everything was just a little different.

There is one area where coordination of the instrumentalists in the pit and vocal forces on stage can be difficult. This problem is in measures where after a fermata or cesura, there is a pick-up beat into the next measure. The singer is going to take a breath before continuing. He will begin on beat four which is the pickup into the following measure. As the conductor, you are sometimes unable to anticipate the singer's breathing in order to cue the orchestra to play exactly when the singer continues. What frequently happens is that the singer begins the pick-up, you cue the orchestra, which plays on your gesture, but the timing is behind that of the singer. There would be no problem in coordinating this situation if the performer were staring directly at the conductor, but that is not what happens in the theatre. It would destroy the mood being created on stage.

One solution to this problem is to have the orchestra eliminate the pick-up by placing a rest on the singer's note and begin playing on the down-beat of the following measure. In the illustration (Example 28-1) the notes marked by "X" will not be played. This will allow the singer to execute the pick-up either on your cue or when they wish to continue, and everyone will be together on beat one, making a clean downbeat. Elimination of all pickups by the orchestra should never be an ironclad rule. But, the removal of many of them will result in tight coordination between the pit and the stage. With practice, experienced pit players will grasp this type of situation and automatically adjust to these problem places.

Example 28-1.
Illustration of a Pick-Up Measure
from "Ballad" from *Beach Journey*

Chapter 29

Tech Rehearsal

The tech (technical) rehearsal, also referred to as a cue-to-cue (Q-2-Q) or a running rehearsal, is exactly what it says. It is a time for dealing with all technical matters on the stage as well as backstage. Time here is spent on making sure the lights have been focused correctly, the placing of scenery and set pieces, the running of scene shifts, and that sort of thing. There can be tech rehearsals with actors as well as without them. If no actors are called in for the tech rehearsal (some refer to this as a dry tech), it will be a rehearsal which is centered around the calls made by the stage manager for lights, sound, shifting of scenery, etc. The director may or may not be present.

If actors are called for a tech (sometimes referred to as a wet tech), all members of the production team are present. The director and choreographer sit in the auditorium and view the production from the hall. The director will communicate with the stage manager, lighting designer and sound engineer through an in-house communication system. If the director needs to speak to the entire company he will use what is sometimes called the "God Mike." This is a loudspeaker system that allows him to make announcements to everyone involved based on his perspective of sitting in the auditorium.

The cue-to-cue or tech rehearsal with actors is a time when an entire scene is rarely run in its entirety. Rather, one goes from one cue to another cue playing only the portion of the scene needed between the cues. If the rehearsal space is a different size than the stage, the director may need to adjust the position of the actors. The choreographer will want to see an entire dance number. If the entire number is not run, positions of the dancers at certain places in the music will be called to be sure that everyone is spaced correctly on the stage. This is not the time for costumes to be tried out, but there could be an exception in some situations. A tech rehearsal is *not* the time for the full orchestra to be present in the pit, as they could spend much of their time waiting for adjustments to be made on stage. The only musician needed in the pit during a tech rehearsal is the rehearsal accompanist along with the musical director. During the cue-to-cue, the musical director may discover that the scene change music is not sufficient, or is too long. He will inform the orchestra if adjustments to the music are necessary prior to the dress rehearsal.

Professional actors will have experienced a technical rehearsal and understand the procedure. It may be necessary to explain the purpose of this rehearsal period to amateur cast members, especially if there seem to be many repetitions of a scene or musical number, in order to assure proper timing of all technical matters with action on the stage. If singers must repeat sections several times, full-voice singing is to be avoided unless one is determining balance or making a microphone check.

A tech rehearsal can take a long time. It can be a frustrating experience for everyone. But, it is rehearsal time that is absolutely necessary in order to work out all the factors of stage coordination. This is the time to work out and solve these problems so that the dress rehearsal will go smoothly and be more successful.

Chapter 30

Dress Rehearsal

The dress rehearsal is exactly what the name indicates—the time to run the show exactly the way the audience will see it. The cast is in costume and make-up, the sets, props, and lights are the way they will be in performance, and the orchestra is in place. During dress rehearsals, as in performances, the musical director is a very busy person. He is involved with the music in the pit as well as with the action on stage because it is your job to coordinate these areas.

During dress rehearsals, the director will sit in the auditorium watching and taking notes that will be given to you as well as to the cast members after the rehearsal is completed. The choreographer is in the auditorium as well, making notes for the dancers and may have a note for you regarding dance tempi. One hopes that the dress rehearsal will be a run-through of the show free of technical problems. This is rarely the case, especially at the first dress rehearsal. A scene shift may go awry, an actor finds a costume change takes longer than planned, the cut in the music that the orchestra previously played quite successfully falls apart, or a singer misses your cue and falls a measure behind the orchestra. The biggest flaw is usually that of sound balance because the orchestra is playing too loudly.

The director will determine the number of dress rehearsals that are necessary and will have indicated these dates on the schedule. These could vary from one to a whole week depending upon the situation. The aim is always same—to run the show without interruption in preparation for the first performance in front of an audience. At the end of a dress rehearsal there is a time for notes.

You will need to give notes to the orchestra as well as to the cast members. At the end of a dress rehearsal it is common to hold the instrumentalists for a brief period of time in order to give your notes to them as a group. You may need to correct wrong notes, clarify how you are conducting a particular passage, or remind the orchestra how their music fits into a particular number. These note-times are critical and not to be taken lightly. Your function here is to correct problems that occurred during the rehearsal and solve these problems before the next dress rehearsal. Even though the orchestra may be tired from just playing a run-through, it will be necessary to repeat musical passages for corrections. And, this is part of the business of getting it right!

How can you make the notes for the cast or orchestra and conduct at the same time? One way is to have a helper, a student or colleague, sit in the pit with you. When you need to correct a wrong note, or notice a musical problem, call out the measure number where the problem occurred, or what the problem was to the person, who will write down what you say. If no one is available to do this, a small tape recorder will serve the same purpose. Speak into the microphone about the note you would have written down. Play the tape either at intermission or at the end of the run-through. After the rehearsal, you will have a list of things to pass on to the orchestra, or to the cast.

A colleague has another solution for remembering where items need to be addressed. He tells me that when a mistake or problem occurs during the rehearsal, he turns down the corner of the page where the error happened. He finds that it is faster than writing notes, where he would have to stop conducting to write, or than speaking into a microphone. And, he finds that just by looking at the page following the run, the problem comes back to him and he can inform the orchestra or cast of the problem. He gives notes to the orchestra before dismissing them and turns up the page indicating the problem has been addressed. If the note be for a cast member, he leaves the page turned down for the meeting where notes are given to the cast. I have adopted his practice of turning down the corner of the page as well as marking the problem measure with an "X" in pencil. When the note has been given to either the cast or the orchestra, I erase the mark. Maybe you have found a better way to remember where places need to be corrected. Whatever method you choose, the point remains the same. You want to stay involved with the run-through, yet be able to give yourself some hint in order to recall a mistake that needs to be corrected.

If you have an assistant who is capable, let him conduct a dress rehearsal, or perhaps a portion of it. This will allow you to sit in the auditorium and to hear as well as see what is going on. Sitting in the theatre will give one a different perspective on the show.

Following run-throughs and dress rehearsals it is customary for the cast to have a meeting where notes are given. This is the time for the director to remind cast members of their blocking, their lines, or their acting. There can be technical notes for the stage manager to deliver to the running crew in order to improve the performance, costumes, lighting, or props. It is also the time when the musical director and choreographer are given a chance to talk with the cast about things that went right or wrong in the rehearsal just completed. This note-time is very important, especially during the dress rehearsal period when the cast is adjusting to the presence of the orchestra as well as to sets and costumes.

It may be necessary to have an additional rehearsal prior to the next dress rehearsal to tighten up a particular musical portion of the show. If there is a chorus master, this person may be able to take this rehearsal. If not, a special time will need to be arranged. Usually a good time is fifteen minutes or half-hour before the sign-in call. Have the necessary people meet to run through the music that has caused the problem.

Once the show is in production, you can take care of quick corrections for the orchestra at the very end of a performance when most of the audience have left the theatre. There may be situations when it is not necessary to give notes to the entire orchestra, but to specific players. This can be done by leaving a written note on their music stand indicating specific places in the score that need attention. Or, you may wish to speak to the woodwinds, or the brass as a section. This can be done in the pit before the house opens or in some convenient location such as the Green Room prior to curtain. A note does not always have to be a problem. It can be a word of thanks for a good performance! Sometimes we accept good playing as the norm, and forget to pass on thanks and congratulations.

It is not uncommon for the musical director to visit back stage prior to dress rehearsal or a performance to give individual cast members reminders or suggestions to the cast. In these instances, the note usually concerns a matter that might have been overlooked at the notes meeting following the previous night's rehearsal. Or it could be a word of encouragement to the cast members that their work the previous night had been excellent and you are encouraging them to continue. Here you probably feel more like an athletic coach urging the team to play their best! But is the situation really any different? One needs to keep in mind that in professional theatre, Equity rules prevent oral or written notes being given to actors after the half-hour call, or thirty minutes before curtain (Equity Handbook, Section 37, Paragraph G).

One final suggestion: We have heard all sorts of tales about dress rehearsals that last for hours and go into the wee hours of the morning. Somehow, it needs to be made perfectly clear to the members of the orchestra just how long they are to be engaged to play for a dress rehearsal. And these terms must be agreed upon by the director. However, in the crunch of a dress rehearsal that extends longer than the agreed upon time, there needs to be some rule that states just how long the orchestra needs to be in place. One student production comes to mind when the rehearsal had lasted long past the agreed upon time, and the players were very tired. Yet no one felt they could tell the conductor what time it was. The concertmaster, a graduate student, took it upon himself to announce to the conductor that the orchestra would play for five more minutes and then would leave. They did, even though the rehearsal was not completed. To my knowledge no one's grade suffered because of this action.

In the professional world, union rules state the length of the rehearsal period. If it extends by even one minute, overtime pay kicks in. No producer/

director wants to incur this additional expenses. The same goes for the amount of time actors can be called before overtime wages go into effect. Plus, there are rules indicating when breaks must be observed.

It is the orchestra in the amateur productions that has no protection from excessively long rehearsals. It is a difficult concept for some directors to understand that the orchestra personnel has agreed to play for rehearsals and performances based upon the schedule that has been posted. Nor, do they understand the physical and mental fatigue factor involved in playing musical instruments. As musical director, you can enforce the schedule by making it clear to the director that the orchestra will be dismissed at a certain time and firmly stick to your statement. Your players will appreciate your consideration for their well-being. And, you might make a point that it is a waste of time to have the orchestra in place before technical problems are solved.

Chapter 31

Performance

The weeks of rehearsals are finished. The dress rehearsals have gotten better with each succeeding night. Now it is time to open the doors to an audience and share with the world what has been taking place all these weeks.

And now the musical director has something new added to his conducting assignment: the pacing of the show. "Pacing can be defined as the correct rhythm for the show regardless of the genre" (Hustoles, 382). Farcical shows move more quickly than other types, which move more leisurely. This variation is because of the differences in the plot. By pacing, I am referring to the movement within the show from one section to the next. We all want the audience to react—laugh, applaud, to savor certain moments. Time needs to be given for this expression of appreciation. Waiting for the crest of the audience's applause after a solo or a chorus number is essential before beginning the next musical item. It is just as important for the actors to hold for the audience's reaction in order that the next line not be stepped-on by laughter. Listening for the applause, finding that peak, learning to hear it begin to diminish so that you know the time is right to continue with the next number comes with experience. Pacing of a show is just as crucial as setting the right tempo for a dance number.[14]

Another area for pacing the show is in the scene changes, which seem to take years during the early dress rehearsals. By opening night, these changes will run more smoothly and by the closing performance they will be almost lightning speed! Cues to stop playing when the lights come up, or to keep playing while the set is changing demands an alert conductor as well as an orchestra that will respond accordingly. Sometimes during a set change, a problem with a set piece may occur. It is an exception to the normal way things run. But, the conductor must be alert to just this type of situation.

Shows that run for a number of performances can get tired and stale. One way of keeping performers on their toes is to give notes to the specific cast members as well as to the instrumentalists. This can be done at the end of a performance, or prior to the next show. Notes from a musical director should be real musical items and not imaginary things. The director, choreographer and the stage manager may give notes during the run of a show. Notes might be, "You were late for your entrance into the song," or "You skipped a beat in such and such a place last night." It is also good to say, "Your number went the best ever last night. Congratulations!" The director could have requested a change which may mean a new repeat in the music, or a quicker tempo. Whatever the note, it is always the aim to strive for better and better performances. At all times, the conductor needs to keep a very alert ear for any deviation in the music and to pass this information to the performers using one's best professional and tactful manner.

Pit deportment is an area of grave concern to the conductor, the cast, and the audience. This is particularly important with amateur players who are new to pit playing, but it can be an issue even in professional situations. It is expected that everyone will be on time, be in place, be warmed up, ready to play, and ready for the down beat at the announced time. This even refers to the orchestra returning in a timely fashion after intermission.

The singers and actors have worked a long time to learn and perfect the show. The instrumentalists probably have not spent the same amount of time on their parts and it is possible that they may not have the same attitude or devotion to the performance. At the first dress rehearsal, the orchestra will want to know what is taking place on the stage and how their music fits in. If the orchestra space allows, they will want to watch the stage. If they have attended the last rehearsal before going on stage, the orchestra will have opportunity to become acquainted with the story.

It is assumed that the first requirement of every pit member should be to play their best. It is also important that they consider themselves as an integral part of the production. They are part of the total performance, not just accompaniment for musical numbers.

If the performance takes place in a theatre where the pit is in full view of the performers on stage, the musicians will need to keep their movement to a minimum in order to avoid distracting the performers who are on stage. When the orchestra can be seen by the audience, such as in a gymnasium where the orchestra may be off to one side, the players should be cautioned about moving and talking among themselves or doing anything that could draw focus from the stage. My dictum to novice players is that the audience paid to see the show on the stage, not the one in the pit! The musicians should not be allowed to whisper to each other or exchange knowing looks when an actor stumbles over a line. This type of behavior is rude and unprofessional. The orchestra is an integral part of the production, even when they are out of the sightline of the audience.

You may have attended a professional production, perhaps one that has been running for several months or even years, and noticed that when the orchestra is not playing, the musicians are doing other things, such as doing a crossword, knitting, or reading. Is this permissible? In amateur or semi-professional productions, absolutely not! You must constantly remind the musicians to stay alert and to be a part of the total performance. I will confess that in semi-professional situations, with shows that have run two weeks or longer, I have not objected when orchestra members have read. However, the rule has been strongly stated from the beginning that they must never, never, ever miss a downbeat. And, they are warned that it is not the conductor's duty to get everyone's attention prior to a musical number. It is the instrumentalists responsibility to always be ready.

Chapter 32

Opening Night

You are now ready for the opening performance and the run of the show, be it for one performance, a weekend of performances, a run of a couple of weeks, or more. Your cast has been given a call and notified when they should arrive for make-up and dressing. The musicians need to have their call time as well. Call time for the orchestra is usually thirty minutes before curtain.

A sign-up board for the orchestra members is a requirement. Just as there is a sign-in sheet for the cast located near the stage door entrance or the dressing room area, there should be a sign-in board for the orchestra. This could be located near the place where the instrumentalists will leave their cases and personal belongings. As the conductor, you do not want to spend your minutes prior to curtain wondering if all your musicians are present. A sign-in board lets you know this. If you have a pit manager, checking the sign-in board to make sure everyone has arrived is one of their major responsibilities.

Your musicians need to have a place to store music cases, as well as any personal items. Professional theatres provide locker space for their musicians. Having a safe storage area will eliminate excess clutter in the pit. The orchestra needs an area where each member can spend some time warming up. After signing in, warming up, and checking for any last minute instructions, the orchestra should be in their places in the pit no later than ten minutes before curtain.

Some situations will not have adequate warm-up places for the instrumentalists, so they will do this in hallways or empty corners. Some players like to warm-up in the room where they will be performing. In this situation, make arrangements to use the pit area prior to the opening of the house. Obviously, it is preferable to have a warm-up area other than the pit in the theatre. No member of the audience wants to be accosted by instrumental chaos while they are settling into their seats and glancing through their programs. That is why all of the warm-ups should take place prior to the opening of the house or in a separate location.

At the latest, players should be in their places ten minutes to curtain. This allows time to check their stand lights and look over their music. If you have left notes for them on their stands, this will give them time to read and check the passages indicated in their parts. About five minutes before curtain, they should make the final tuning, and then be quiet for the remainder of the time before the cue to begin the performance. This cue is often the dimming of the house lights or at the end of some announcement regarding the policy of photography and the use of recording devices.

I like to arrive at the theatre between thirty to forty-five minutes prior to curtain. This allows for time to meet with any of the cast members, or check for any notes that might have been left by the director or the stage manager regarding the previous night's performance. I also put my score on the podium and check my stand light. I take the baton from its case and place it on the open score. About twenty minutes before curtain, I check with the pit manager to see if there is anything I should know. This also allows ample time to check with the musicians for any last minute details or notes from the previous performance or rehearsal. By five to eight minutes before curtain, I am in place at the podium sitting in the conductor's chair. If a headset is provided, I can check with the stage manager for any last minute details such as if there will be any delays in curtain time.

The stage manager is responsible for giving the time count-down to the cast before calling "places." This count-down usually begins with a thirty minute call which is often coupled with the announcement that the "House is open." These time-to-curtain announcements continue back stage at five to ten minute intervals. When the announcement "Five minutes to curtain" is given to the cast, I hear this on my headset and pass this information on to the orchestra, as a notice for any last-minute adjustments that might need to be completed. The five-minute warning is a notice that things are about to happen. When the stage manager calls, "We are at places," I relay this information to the orchestra as well. The downbeat to the start of the show is imminent. If the conductor has not stood up in his place, this is the time to do so. If you are on headset, you will hear the stage manager calling for various pre-curtain activities, such as the dimming of the houselights, the fading of the warmers on the curtains, and other pre-curtain raising announcements. If there is an extended overture, this will begin when the house is dark. And the raising of the curtain will come from a cue in the music. Otherwise, the raising of the curtain and the starting of the show could begin at the same time if there is little or no pre-curtain music. If a headset arrangement between stage manager and the pit is not possible, the cue for the conductor to get ready for the overture could be the dimming of the houselights to half. When the house is dark, you can begin the music. Regardless of how it is done, those last minutes of countdown prior to the starting of the overture can be as exciting as a space launch!

The dress for the orchestra should be dark, comfortable, appropriate, yet unobtrusive. Not every theatre has a pit which is low enough for the orchestra to be out of sight. Or, perhaps you are performing in a makeshift facility where the orchestra is on the same level as the audience, either directly in front of the stage or off to the side. Darker clothing aids in blending in with the blackouts and will not stand out when the stage is dark. Formal wear, such as tuxes for men and black dresses for women, is appropriate, and is used in many places, as it sets the tone of the evening. However, black shirts and trousers for men and similar attire for women is perhaps more comfortable. This type of outfit is worn by the orchestra players in New York, so why not copy their practice. For a recent New York performance of *1776,* the orchestra was behind the set and could not be seen. After the performance you could tell who was in the orchestra as they were the people carrying instrument cases out of the theatre. Their dress for the show was jeans and sweatshirts!

Light bleeding from the stand lights is always a problem in orchestra pits that are not specifically designed for theatre productions. The customary black metal stands with clip-on stand lights may require a gel taped over the light so that it is not too bright. This also reduces the light that shines on the musician's music. If the pit is constructed correctly, this will not be a problem. Some places have special box-like stands where the light shines on the music but the sides of the stand are high enough to prevent light from bleeding into the hall. Some productions require that stand lights be turned off at certain places to assure complete darkness on the stage. If this is required, there is usually a master switch which controls all the lights to accomplish this task.

It is not uncommon for the lightbulb on a music stand to go out during a performance. Keeping a bag of spare bulbs in the pit can solve the emergency when one of your players cannot see the music! Let your pit members know that extra bulbs are available in case of such an event and that they are located either with the conductor or with the pit manager. It is nice when the light goes out during a dialog passage and a new bulb can be passed to the dark stand. It is more likely that this is going to happen during some crucial musical passage! The player may be able to continue using the light that falls on his music from the stage. If this is not the case, they will probably just have to wait until a spare bulb can be passed to them during the next passage of dialog.

The conductor may wish to meet with the principals and chorus prior to the performance for vocal warm-ups or last minute instructions. This is particularly important on opening night when everyone is wishing everyone else a "good show," or "break a leg." It is equally good to meet with the cast on following nights, especially if you as conductor have a note for a particular performer or the cast as a whole. This meeting time is also a good time to share compliments from the previous evening's performance, as well as alert the cast for places that were rough in the previous night's performance. Warm-ups can be conducted by a member of the cast who has been appointed as chorus master, just as dance warm-ups are under the supervision of the dance captain.

Some performance spaces may require the conductor to make a formal entrance to the pit. Other places may expect the conductor to be in place and just begin the overture on cue. If the conductor must make a formal entrance from outside the auditorium into the pit, the stage manager will give the cue to enter. The conductor should enter the pit with a follow-spot and acknowledge the applause of the audience, get into place quickly, and begin the overture. Remember, the audience did not pay money to see you walk in! Many theatres do not make a practice of highlighting the conductor's entry, but merely shine a spotlight on the conductor during the playing of the overture. If the conductor makes an entrance prior to the second act, this would be an appropriate time for the recognition of the instrumentalists. If so, have them stand, quickly acknowledge them and get on with the business of playing the entr'acte music.

It is customary that the conductor and orchestra be acknowledged at the end of the performance. This is done during the bow music. This acknowledgment is a gesture given by the principals by pointing to the conductor at which time a spotlight is shone on the conductor. Provided the playing of the bow music will not fall apart if the conductor stops beating time, he can acknowledge this gesture by turning and bowing to the audience. Over the years, it has been my practice to return the cast's acknowledgment with a wave of my own back to them. Sometimes, I have turned around, quickly bowed to the audience and then returned to conducting the bows and exit music. It has varied depending on the music being conducted at the time of the gesture. In any case, one should do what is comfortable.

Chapter 33

After the Last Performance

The show is closing. Your run of performances is completed. However, your responsibilities did not end with the last note of the exit music. All rented material must be collected so that it can be returned to the licensing agency. The actors are required to erase all marks made in their scripts and return this material to the stage manager. The actor's materials are commonly collected when the show goes into performances.

The rented materials used by the orchestra are collected after the final performance of the show. It is best to try and collect this music before any one leaves the orchestra pit, as this will save running down a score that someone has taken with them. It is each player's responsibility to erase all the marks they made in the music during rehearsals or performances. This must be done before the music can be returned to the rental library. You may either require the instrumentalists to do their own erasing, or appoint a student(s) or your assistant to do this when the parts are turned in. In any case, expect to have parts returned promptly and erased.

I prefer to have all the music returned to the pit manager or the musical director after the final performance. If for some reason it is not possible to have the music at that time, you must expect the music to be in your hands within twelve to twenty-four hours. The reason for this urgency is that all music and scripts must be returned to the licensing agency within five working days of the last performance, otherwise there is a hefty charge levied for late return. Be sure to make it quite clear that if any one returns a score after the materials have been shipped, that late fee becomes the responsibility of the musician, not the organization that produced the show. Perhaps this is why final paychecks of the musicians are held until all the music has been returned.

There are other end of show duties. There will need to be a break down in the pit similar to the striking of the set on the stage of all equipment used by the orchestra. Where do the chairs go? What happens to the music stands and stand lights? Who collects the extension chords? Where is all the percussion equipment to be stored? The pit area must be cleaned, swept, and all trash removed that might have accumulated during the performances. This cleaning up is a excellent job for the pit manager or the assistant to the musical director to supervise. Regardless of who supervises or does the work, it is in the musical director's job description to see that everything is left as tidy and as it was found.

If your orchestra players were salaried, be sure that they are paid the agreed upon amount at the agreed upon time. If there is some variation of the payment date from what is in the contract, be sure that it is clear when they are to receive their check. They probably will play better if all this information is clear from the beginning.

I think it is a good manners to thank each musician personally for their work on the show and invite them to play in future pits, especially if you have been pleased with their work. After all, you have been a tightly knit group for several evenings. A Tootsie Roll left on each music stand is a small way of saying "thank you." Another way could be to send out for a pizza for all to share when the pit has been restored to its proper order.

After the last performance of a show's run, I try to shake hands with every musician and verbally express my thanks personally for their work. A written note of thanks or even a general letter addressed to everyone in the pit is another way of showing your appreciation. The thank-you note/letter is more than an expression of etiquette. It can also be a time when the conductor can share some musical insights. Robert Shaw's letters to his singers during the Collegiate Chorale era expressed more than his evaluation of their performance. These "Dear People" letters have become the written record of this great conductor's musical philosophy.

Chapter 34

Is Pit Playing Hack Work?

I am very well aware that there are some instrumentalists who make it a practice never to play in any pit, whether it be musical theatre or opera. This decision is their privilege. I know many applied teachers who discourage their students from ever taking part in this experience, as they feel the students could be spending their time much better through practice or learning other literature. I do not disagree with these worthwhile pursuits, but in the real world, many musicians find that playing in a pit orchestra provides them with an opportunity to earn some extra money. They also find that they gain valuable musical experience by doing this type of work. For younger instrumentalists, pit playing will be a completely different musical experience from playing for football half-time shows or formal band/orchestra concerts. Through a pit experience, young instrumentalists "will enjoy being associated with a musical production and will become more flexible, responsive musicians in a variety of other performance situations" (Rosewell 1981, 53). I do not think anyone should ever consider pit playing as being beneath their musical skills. To do this job well requires too many demands on one's musicianship.

It is my opinion that good pit playing is an art that can be related to performing chamber music. Why? First, each musician must be totally competent and in control of his own instrument, as in any one-to-a-part chamber music situation. Second, each musician must listen not only to his own part but to what is going on around him and know how his part fits into the whole musical picture, just as in any chamber music situation. The third point is the unique part of this discussion. In addition to being competent on their instrument, and listening to the other players in the ensemble, members of the pit orchestra have the added responsibility of knowing what is taking place on stage. And it is this third area of listening that stretches every musician's ear.

It is this three-faceted approach to performance that places a tremendous responsibility on the instrumentalist. As has been mentioned earlier, alert pit members have saved many a performance from disaster. By their alertness, they were able to make adjustments in the music and coincide with the action taking place on the stage more quickly than a conductor could announce the solution. Therefore, a good pit player is a true chamber musician!

Chapter 35

Well . . . Maybe Next Time

Well! You got through it. You did a good job, and you had fun. Before you know it, you are already thinking about the next production! You are remembering what went well with the show you just conducted, and what could have been improved. You might be thinking about how much easier the next show will be because you have already been through the routine once. You may not feel like a pro, but you are certainly no longer a rank beginner. The musical theatre bug has bitten many people, sometimes with a ferocious bite.

Take it from someone who has had the opportunity to be on the stage and knows about the "smell of the greasepaint." There can be an equally fatal "smell of the pit." In its own special way, this work can be as satisfying to be below the stage in front of the footlights as it is to be on the stage behind the footlights. The musical director and orchestra are not always recognized in the newspaper reviews with the same glowing terms as are the actors. And sometimes the audience will forget to express their appreciation to you. But they will be aware of your presence—especially if you play too loudly. Despite the hours of hard work, the weeks of rehearsals, and the frustrations when things do not go the way you had planned, being a musical director is just about the "most fun thing" in the world! "So don't hold back . . . get in there and do it. It's worth it" (Lee 48).

Welcome to the joys of being a musical director!

Appendix

Licensing Agents

Music Theatre International
421 W. 54th St.
New York, NY 10019

Rogers & Hammerstein Theatre Library
229 W. 28th St.
New York, NY 10001

Samuel French, Inc.
45 W. 25th St.
New York, NY 10010

Tams-Witmark Music Library
560 Lexington Avenue
New York, NY 10022

Notes

1. In a recent conversation with a professional musical director from Chicago about how we both had gotten into this crazy business, she commented, "There is nothing out there written on this subject. And, there needs to be."

2. The masculine gender is used throughout this book in order to avoid the "he/she" or person/people situation in order to avoid sexist language. In every case, unless specified, both males and females are meant. Nowhere is the use of the masculine pronouns intended to exclude females, whose work has been so important to the theatre, from this discussion.

3. Additional information on the production staff along with an organizational flow chart can be found in the chapter, "Production Staff for Musicals," in Laughlin & Wheeler's *Producing the Musical,* 14. Another example is found in the "Production Organization Chart" in Boland and Argentini's, *Musicals!*, 21.

4. Regarding the role of the producer, Engle states in his book:

> A producer may not be employed in all nonprofessional theaters. However, an equivalent position must exist. The first thing anyone needs to learn about theater (musical theater in particular, since it involves participation by so many people) is that it is not, never has been, and never can be a democratic institution. It cannot be run successfully by vote. Productions must be "governed" from a single point of view, and every participant must be willing to adhere to the dictates of one person at the top. This person—with or without a title—is indeed the producer. He has the vision, the know-how to run things, and, if he is frustrated or interfered with, his vision will become confused and the resultant production must suffer.
>
> After all, it *is* the producer's responsibility not only to approve the choice of the show he plans to mount, but to oversee casting; approve the director's and choreographer's work-in-progress; consent to the director's scenic preferences; observe the musical director's progress; and regulate the dozens of other operations that can contribute significantly to his project, the success or failure of which will reflect on him (Engle 1983, 5, 6).

5. For a practical introduction to the role of the choreographer in theatre, see Mary C. Robare, *Five, Six, Seven, Eight, Dance! Music Theatre Choreography.* Warrenton, VA: Society for Applied Learning, 2000. This CD/ROM gives text as well as movement illustrations.

6. For an historical survey of the changing role of the chorus and its function in musical theatre, see the excellent discussion in DeLorenzo's dissertation, *The Chorus in American Musical Theatre.*

7. A thorough discussion dealing with the process of selecting a work is found in Laughlin and Wheeler, *Producing the Musical,* pages 26-28. There are other sources available dealing with this subject, such as the catalogs of the four licensing agencies.

8. An example of a sample card for audition rating is found in Hawthorne, *There's More to Musicals Than Music,* 8; as well as in Laughlin and Wheeler, *Producing the Musical*, 31.

9. A colleague addresses this problem in this way. The students are encouraged to learn the music the way it is performed on the recording. As musical director, he makes the final decision based on whether the student is successful performing the song in that manner, or if they should restrict their singing to what is found on the printed page.

10. An excellent discussion dealing with the subject of the belt voice and the legit voice, as well as the in-between-voice is found in Citron, *The Musical From the Inside Out*, 77-78.

11. The following contains some of this confusing terminology:

Theatrical Logic
In is down, down is front
Out is up and up is back
Off is out, on is in
And of course, left is right and right is left
A drop shouldn't and a
Block and fall does neither
A prop doesn't and
A cove has no water
Tripping is OK
A running crew rarely gets anywhere
A purchase line buys you nothing
A trip will not catch anything
A gridiron has nothing to do with football
Strike is work (in fact, a lot of work)
And a green room, thank God, usually isn't
Now that you're versed in theatrical terms,
Break a leg
But not really . . .

On Cue, The Actors' Center Newsletter, September 1999, 6

12. For more about phrase length, see Citron, *The Musical From the Inside Out,* 77. He also discusses the form of songs in musicals, ABA, AABA, etc. which is very helpful. In fact, the chapter entitled "Basic Training" is most interesting and helpful, as is the entire book.

13. For more on the vamp from a performer's point of view, see discussion in Craig, *On Singing Onstage*, 71.

14. While in graduate school, my organ teacher and I had a running disagreement regarding the correct tempo for playing hymns. I complained that he played hymns too slowly. He insisted that the most important factor in hymn playing was not how fast or slow a hymn was played, but the pacing—how one went from verse to verse. It took me years to understand what he meant. In addition to being an excellent organist, this teacher was a superb accompanist who also accompanied for music theatre. Could it all be related?

Bibliography

Although a great deal of the discussion concerning the job of a musical director has been based upon personal experience gained from working in musical theatre at Shenandoah University, Winchester, Virginia, there are several sources that have been consulted which make reference to musical aspects of theatre. These will supplement and broaden one's knowledge of the theatre art.

Berkson, Robert. *Musical Theatre Choreography.* London: A & C Black, 1990.

Boland, Robert, and Paul Argentini. *Musicals!* Lanham, Md.: Scarecrow Press, 1997.

Bunn, Michael. Conversation with author. 16 May 1998.

Citron, Stephen. *The Musical From the Inside Out.* Chicago: Ivan R. Dee, 1992.

Craig, David. *On Singing Onstage.* New York: Applause Theatre Book, 1978, 1990.

DeLorenzo, Joseph P. "The Chorus in American Musical Theatre." Ph.D. diss. New York University, 1985.

Engel, Lehman. *The American Musical Theater.* New York: Collier Books, 1967, 1975.

_______. *Getting the Show On.* New York: Schirmer Books, 1983.

_______. *Planning and Producing the Musical Show.* New York: Crown Publishers, 1966.

Equity Handbook. Actors' Equity Association, (n.d.) (n.p.).

"Finally in Finale." *MTI Times*, winter, 1997.

Fisher, Marc. "Performance Assessment." *The Washington Post Magazine,* 23 April 2000.

Grote, David. *Staging the Musical.* New York: Prentice Hall, 1986.

Hamlisch, Marvin, and Edward Klebar. *A Chorus Line.* New York: Tams Witmark, 1975, 1977.

Hare, Walter Ben. *The Minstrel Encyclopedia.* Boston: Walter H. Baker, 1926.

Hawthorne, Grace, comp. *There's More to Musicals Than Music.* Carol Stream, Ill.: Somerset Books, 1980.

Heier, James O. "It's Not 'the Pits.'" *Music Educators Journal* 70, nl (September 1983) 43.

Herman, Harold. Personal interview. 21 November 1997.

Hoare, William. *The Musical Director in the Amateur Theatre.* Malvern, Worcestershire, England: J. Garnet Miller, 1993.

Hustoles, Paul J. "Musical Theatre Directing: A Generic Approach." Ph.D. diss. Texas Tech University, 1984.

Laughlin, Haller, and Randy Wheeler. *Producing the Musical.* Westport, Conn.: Greenwood Press, 1984.

Lee, Marcella. "How to Produce a Successful High School Musical." *Music Educators Journal* 70, n1 (September 1983): 40-48.

Miller, Bruce. "The Singing Audition." *Dramatics* 71, n5 (January 2000): 26-31.

Miller, Leon. *How to Direct the High School Play*. Chicago: The Dramatic Publishing Company, 1968.

Music Theatre International. *Catalog Supplement, 1997*. New York, 1997.

Myers, Judy. Personal interview. 2 July 1999.

Nelson, Richard. "Conducting Problems in the Production of a Broadway Musical for a Community Theater." Master's thesis, San Jose State University, 1976.

Oliver, Donald. *How to Audition for the Musical Theatre*. New York: Drama Book Publishers, 1985.

On Cue! Arlington, Va.: The Actors' Center Newsletter, September 1999.

Packer, Ginny. "Putting on the Musical—Junior High Style." *Choral Journal* 5, 27 (March 1986) 21-23.

Paull, Barbara, and Christine Harrison. *The Athletic Musician*. Lanham, Md.: Scarecrow Press, 1997.

Ratliff, Gerald Lee, and Suzanne Trauth. *On Stage: Producing Musical Theatre*. New York: Rosen Publishing Group, 1988.

Read, Gardner. *Music Notation*. 2nd edition. New York: Taplinger Publishing, 1979.

Rodgers and Hammerstein Theatre Library, 1998 edition, (n.p., n.d.).

Rosewall, Ellen. "Teaching the Musical Theatre Style." *National Association of Teachers of Singing Bulletin* 37, n2 (1980): 17-18.

Rosewall, Ellen W. "Your Role in the Musical Comedy Production." *Music Educators Journal* 68, n2 (October 1981): 52-53.

Ross, Beverly B., and Jean P. Durgin. *Junior Broadway*. Jefferson, N.C.: McFarland, 1983.

Silver, Fred. *Auditioning for the Musical Theatre*. New York: New Market Press, 1985.

________. "Auditioning for the Musical Theater." *The Back Stage Handbook for Performing Artists*. Compiled and edited by Sherry Eaker. New York: Back Stage Books, 1989.

Stearns, David Patrick. "'West Side Story' Between Broadway and the Opera House." Liner notes. *Leonard Bernstein conducts West Side Story*. CD. Deutsche Grammophone, 1985.

Stegall, June. Telephone conversation. 10 January 2000.

________. Interview. 4 April 2000.

Tiboris, Peter. "Producing Musical Theatre: Some Recommended Readings." *Choral Journal* 21, 7 (March 1981): 19-21.

Toby's Dinner Theatre: Advertisement. *Washington Post*, 8 August 1999, G-7.

Tumbusch, Tom. *The Theatre Student's Complete Production Guide to Modern Musical Theatre*. New York : Richards Rosen Press, 1969.

Wenger Music Facility Equipment 1998-1999. Owatonna, Minn., 1998.

White, Matthew. *Staging a Musical*. New York: Routledge, 1999.

Wolfe, John Leslie. Email to author. 3 January 2000.

Young, David. *How to Direct a Musical*. New York: Routledge, 1995.

Index

About the Author

James H. Laster is Professor Emeritus at Shenandoah Conservatory of Shenandoah University, Winchester, Virginia, where he has taught since 1973. He has been the musical director for over fifty musical theatre productions, and has appeared on stage in roles such as F. Alexander in *A Clockwork Orange*, the Resident in *Indian Ink,* the Provost in Shakespeare's *Measure for Measure,* Pellinor in *Camelot*, Col. Pickering in *My Fair Lady*, Fodor in *Crazy for You*, and Mr. Brownlow in *Oliver*. Laster holds a B.A. with majors in music history and biology from Maryville College, Maryville, Tennessee; an M.A. in musicology and a Ph.D. in church music from George Peabody College for Teachers, Nashville, Tennessee; a certificate in organ from the Mozarteum Summer-Academy, Salzburg, Austria, and an M.S. in library science (music emphasis) from Catholic University, Washington, D. C., none of which trained or prepared him for this aspect of his life!